- 5 DEC 2011

D0229429

WATERCOLOUR COURSE

Paint a landscape in minutes

SELECT
EDITIONS

WATERCOLOUR COURSE

To Dorothy, my wife, for her support, advice and typing of the text, and to all my students over the years whose needs have helped me to determine the content of this book.

This edition published 2003

Selecta Book
Folly Road, Roundway, Devizes,
Wiltshire SN10 2HR

Copyright © Arcturus Publishing Limited
26/27 Bickels Yard, 151–153 Bermondsey Street,
London SE1 3HA

ISBN 1-84193-186-1

WINSOR & NEWTON, COTMAN, FINITY, SCEPTRE GOLD, WINSOR and the GRIFFIN device are trademarks of ColArt Fine Art & Graphics Limited.

Printed in China

Contents

Throughout its long and successful history, the Winsor & Newton brand has developed a proud tradition of producing fine art materials of the highest quality – the company is delighted to witness the publication of a range of watercolour books that achieves similarly high levels of quality and innovation.

WATERCOLOUR COURSE

INTRODUCTION

Watercolour painting opens up a new world. It is exciting: the unexpected happens, colours blend together to create wonderful effects.

Many people think they can't paint. Well, I say they can. I don't believe painting is a gift. Anyone can be taught to paint. However, whatever we hope to achieve in life, we have to work at it. The same goes for painting. Even if you never reach masterclass level, painting will change your life – Ask any artist. Yes, you will make mistakes; we all do. The secret is to understand what has gone wrong and to learn from your mistakes.

My aim in this book is to save you twenty years of learning, by showing you the techniques, tips and useful practices I have developed over many years of painting and experimentation. I will be showing you how to paint a wide range of outdoor scenes, incorporating the major features found in landscapes: skies, mountains, lakes, trees, rocks, running water, buildings, bridges and walls. In addition I shall be demonstrating how to bring atmosphere and mood to your paintings.

It is not my intention to impose a specific style of painting on you. With practice you will develop your own, and this will become your handwriting in paint, easily recognizable by others as your personal signature.

Learning to paint watercolours is fun, and it's easier than you think. I welcome this opportunity to show you how it's done.

Happy Painting!

Keith H Fenwick

INTRODUCTION

A visit to the local art store can be a confusing experience. My preference is to use quality materials, and I would advise you to do the same. Purchase the best you can afford. It will work out cheaper in the long run and save you a great deal of frustration.

PAINTS

Most professional artists prefer tube colours because they are moist and more convenient for mixing large washes of colour. Pans of paint become very hard if left unused and release less colour.

The choice of colours is personal to the artist, but you won't go far wrong if you begin with my basic range. This comprises:

SKIES
Alizarin Crimson
Cerulean Blue
Cobalt Blue
French Ultramarine
Indanthrene Blue
Payne's Gray
Winsor Red

EARTH
Burnt Sienna
Burnt Umber
Cadmium Yellow Pale
Gold Ochre
Permanent Sap Green
Raw Sienna
Winsor Yellow

ROCKS
Alizarin Crimson
Burnt Sienna
Burnt Umber
Payne's Gray
Raw Sienna

TREES
Alizarin Crimson
Burnt Sienna
Cadmium Yellow Pale
Cerulean Blue
French Ultramarine
Payne's Gray

Permanent Sap Green
Raw Sienna

WATER
Alizarin Crimson
Burnt Umber
Cerulean Blue
French Ultramarine
Payne's Gray

LIGHT
Cadmium Yellow Pale
Gold Ochre
Raw Sienna
White of the paper
Winsor Yellow

ATMOSPHERE AND MOOD
Alizarin Crimson
Burnt Umber
Cerulean Blue
French Ultramarine
Payne's Gray
Raw Sienna

SHADOWS
Alizarin Crimson
Burnt Umber
French Ultramarine
Raw Sienna

BRICKWORK
Burnt Sienna
Cobalt Blue
Raw Sienna
Vermilion

STONEWORK
Alizarin Crimson
Burnt Sienna
Cobalt Blue
Raw Sienna

SPECIAL APPLICATIONS
Gold Ochre
Purple Madder
Winsor Red
Winsor Yellow

PALETTE

All artists have their own way of painting. I prefer to use a large open palette. I simply draw my colours into the centre of the palette and mix them to my requirements. For large washes I premix colours in saucers. The palette shown includes a lid which provides more than ample space for mixing colours.

BRUSHES

For painting skies and other large areas, I use a 1½in hake brush and for control a size 14 round. For buildings and angular elements, such as mountains and rocks, I use a ¾in flat. For fine detail, such as tree structures, I use a size 3 rigger (originally developed for painting ships' rigging, hence the name), and for detailed work (shadows etc) I use a size 6 round.

PAPERS

Quality papers come in different forms, sizes, textures and weights. Paper can also be purchased in gummed pads, spiral bound pads, blocks (glued all around except for an area where the sheets can be separated) and in varying sizes and textures.

I prefer to purchase my paper in sheet form (30in x 22in) and cut it to the appropriate size. The paintings in this book were painted on 200 or 300lb rough textured watercolour paper. When sketching outdoors, I use spiral bound pads.

Winsor & Newton offer a choice of surfaces and weights, as follows:

HP (Hot pressed) has a smooth surface, used for calligraphy and pen and wash.

NOT (Cold pressed) has a slight texture (called 'the tooth') and is used for traditional watercolour paintings.

ROUGH paper has a more pronounced texture which is wonderful for large washes, tree foliage, sparkle on water, dry brush techniques, etc. I always use a rough textured paper.

Paper can be purchased in different imperial weights (the weight of a ream [500 sheets], size 30in x 22in):

90lb/190gsm is thin and light; unless wetted and stretched, it cockles very easily when washes are applied.

140lb/300gsm paper doesn't need stretching unless very heavy washes are applied.

200lb/425gsm or 300lb/640gsm papers are my preference.

OTHER ITEMS

The following items make up my painting kit:

Tissues: For creating skies, applying textures and cleaning palettes.

Mediums: Art Masking Fluid, Permanent Masking Medium, Granulation Medium and Lifting Preparation are all useful and selectively used in my paintings.

Masking tape: To control the flow of paint, masking areas in the painting and for fastening paper to backing board. I prefer ¾in width as it is easier to remove.

Cocktail sticks: Useful for applying masking when fine lines are required.

Grease-proof paper: For applying masking.

Atomizer bottle: For spraying paper with clean water or paint.

Painting board: Your board should be 2 inches larger all round than the size of your watercolour painting. Always secure your paper at each corner and each side (8 places) to prevent it cockling when you are painting.

Eraser: A putty eraser is ideal for removing masking.

Sponge: Natural sponges are useful for removing colour and creating tree foliage, texture on rocks, etc.

Water-soluble crayons: For drawing outlines, correcting mistakes and adding highlights.

Palette knife: For moving paint around on the paper (see page 32).

Saucers: For mixing large washes and pouring paint.

Hairdryer: For drying paint between stages.

Easel and stool: I occasionally use a lightweight easel and a stool for outdoor work.

SKIES, MOUNTAINS & LAKES

PAINTING SKIES *Introduction*

Skies are exciting to paint and they take so little time – less than three minutes. They establish the atmosphere and mood of the painting and, as they can represent up to two-thirds of a painting, it's important to paint them well.

As the weather changes, the sky influences the colours in the landscape. A pale blue sky drenched in sunshine makes the landscape sparkle. When the blue changes to grey, indicating an approaching storm, the landscape colours become dull and moody. A full blown storm creates a sense of fear and awe.

Sometimes there will be no clouds in the sky on the day you have chosen to work outdoors. It's not unusual for me to create an interesting sky to complement my landscape. If nature's perfect, copy it; if it's not, use artistic licence to improve it. Be creative, use your imagination.

Often I will paint the landscape and then paint in the sky to fit it. Acrylic watercolours are particularly useful in this instance, because if the sky colour runs over my under-painting the colour can't be lifted. A big advantage.

In this part of the book my aim is to show you how to paint a wide variety of interesting skies. Skies aren't difficult to paint, but they must be painted quickly. No two artists are ever going to be able to paint identical skies because of the speed at which they have to be painted to avoid hard edges forming – but that's what is so exciting about watercolour painting.

I hope the examples in this book will inspire you. Constant practice will boost your confidence until the painting of skies becomes second nature.

You will call on a range of colours to paint skies. Here are the ones I find most useful:

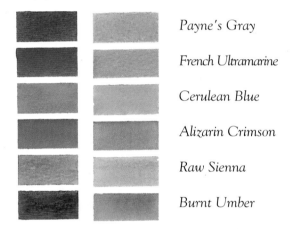

Payne's Gray

French Ultramarine

Cerulean Blue

Alizarin Crimson

Raw Sienna

Burnt Umber

In this sketch I used a very simple technique, creating the cirrus sky by removing paint with an absorbent tissue.

Which cloud?

To identify clouds think descriptively. You might describe the four basic cloud types in these terms:

CIRRUS: hair-like or feathery
CUMULUS: balls of cotton wool
NIMBUS: dark rain-bearing clouds
STRATUS: clouds in layers

This painting provides a good example of a cumulus sky; see page 15 for an explanation of the techniques involved.

TYPES OF CLOUD

More important than being able to identify clouds is to be able to represent them realistically. Observation is important if you are going to make them look real. Let's look at a few of the basic types in more detail:

Cirrus clouds appear as wispy streaks high up in the sky.

Cumulus clouds are soft and fluffy, like balls of cotton wool floating in the sky. They appear larger at the top and smaller at the bottom (in the distance –

perspective). Cumulus clouds display shadows and on a sunny day their tops sparkle with a soft yellow. Their base is usually flat.

Nimbus clouds tell us that a storm is imminent. Dark and rain-bearing, they can fill us with a sense of awe or foreboding.

Stratus clouds, as the name suggests, form in almost horizontal layers across the sky.

11

PAINTING SKIES *Timing*

The sky can represent up to two-thirds of your painting, creating the atmosphere and mood of the landscape. It therefore goes without saying that the ability to paint an interesting sky is important. It's not possible, however, or necessary, to expect to represent the sky exactly – you can't be expected to compete with nature. As artists, our challenge is to paint a believable representation.

Timing is paramount when painting skies. Hard edges, cauliflowers, whatever you want to call them, occur when wet paint is applied over an under-painting that is more than one-third dry. Each successive layer of paint should be stiffer (less wet) than the under-painting. Practise until you've managed to paint a sky in under three minutes without hard edges forming.

This soft sky was painted by initially applying a Raw Sienna wash. The clouds were painted with broad strokes of the 1¹/₂ in hake brush loaded with a Payne's Gray/Cerulean Blue mix. I used a tissue to create a few wispy white clouds.

Painting clouds
When you're painting in clouds, it's a good idea to leave about 50 per cent of your under-painting uncovered.

AVOIDING HARD EDGES

The reason for the formation of hard edges is that wet paint is applied over an under-painting that is more than one-third dry. A simple experiment will show you what an unpleasant effect this creates.

Try it for yourself. Paint in any dark colour, let it partially dry, drop a splash of water in the middle and watch the hard edges form.

The picture shown left is typical of that produced by beginners to watercolour painting who haven't yet mastered the timing. Two things have happened here. Wet paint has been applied over an under-painting that was about half dry, creating the unwanted feather-like hard edges, and the cloud edges haven't softened and been able to blend into the drier under-painting. The result is a messy muddy looking, un-attractive sky. Compare this with the effect achieved in the painting below.

Here the cloud formations were painted when the shine had gone off the under-painting, resulting in a soft, fresh looking, wet into wet sky. To achieve this effect, your sky must be painted in under three minutes.

PAINTING SKIES *Colour mixing*

Each type of sky provides us with an interesting roof to our painting and creates the atmosphere and mood. These will in turn determine the colours and tones we use to paint them.

The colours and mixes shown here are those I most commonly use when painting skies. There may be occasions when I require a particular depth of colour or subtle tone, and in these circumstances I may select additional colours.

Indanthrene Blue mixed with Payne's Gray, for example, produces a deep rich blue. Purple Madder is useful when painting evening skies. I find Raw Sienna invaluable as an initial wash over the paper. It adds warmth to the sky, but apply it as a very pale wash. There is a vast range of colours available, so why not try them.

BRUSHWORK
Use a light touch with a large brush, and the minimum number of brush strokes. If you brush over the under-painting more than is necessary, your sky will look muddy.

The 1½in hake brush is ideal for painting skies. Familiarize yourself with it by using it for the projects on the facing page. Apply bold sweeping strokes with your arm rather than using a wrist action.

To achieve the correct balance of colour you will need to experiment with mixing colours. The mixes shown right are just some of the variations possible using the colours shown below left.

The colours shown below right are mixes useful for clouds and varying strengths of Raw Sienna for under-painting.

Payne's Gray
French Ultramarine
Cerulean Blue
Alizarin Crimson
Raw Sienna
Burnt Umber

Strong colour   Water added

Top row: Payne's Gray and Cerulean Blue – cloud colours
Second row: Payne's Gray and Cerulean Blue – more cloud colours
Third row: Payne's Gray and Alizarin Crimson – cloud colour variations
Fourth row: Raw Sienna – varying strengths for the under-painting

I used a 1½in hake brush to paint this atmospheric sky, applying a weak Raw Sienna wash to the whole of the sky area and quickly washing in some Cerulean Blue at the top right and a weak Alizarin Crimson in selected areas. When the shine had gone from the paper surface (less than one-third dry), I painted in the dark clouds using strong mixes of Payne's Gray/Alizarin Crimson.

For this evening sky, initially I painted Raw Sienna above the horizon line and added some Alizarin Crimson, then immediately I painted the blue sky by brushing in a strong wash of a Payne's Gray/French Ultramarine mix, allowing the paint to run down and blend with the Raw Sienna/Alizarin Crimson washes. A soft tissue was used to remove paint to create the white feathery clouds. A little Cadmium Yellow Pale was used to paint the setting sun.

You'll enjoy painting this sunset using the 1½in hake brush. Initially I applied a Raw Sienna wash to the whole of the sky area and painted in some Cerulean Blue at the top right. The dark clouds were painted using a Payne's Gray/Alizarin Crimson mix, leaving about half of the under-painting showing through.

PAINTING SKIES *Techniques*

Once you have mastered the brush strokes and timing, you will really enjoy painting skies.

All skies are painted wet into wet. This means that you paint wet paint into a wet under-painting. We have already seen how tricky this can be, so always apply the basic principles discussed previously to avoid hard edges. The hake brush is traditionally used for painting skies. I prefer one that has soft hair (goat hair) and is 1½ in wide. The secret when painting skies is to wet your paper initially with clean water or a weak raw sienna. You can apply your wash quickly with sweeping strokes, using arm rather than wrist movements.

Once I see the shine going off the paper I paint in my cloud structures, using a light touch of the hake. Don't brush over the paint too many times. The fewer brush strokes you use, the fresher your sky will look.

Your board should be angled at approximately 15 degrees, just sufficient to allow the paint to run slowly down the paper. Timing comes with experience, so you will need to practise painting lots of skies – after all, they only take three minutes.

The right look

Don't forget, when using watercolours – if it looks right when it's wet, it's wrong! As the paint dries you can lose up to 30 per cent of tonal value, so you must paint with darker tones to allow for this.

I observe this kind of sky most evenings when I look out of my window. I painted a Cadmium Yellow Pale wash, adding Raw Sienna and Alizarin Crimson to produce a variegated under-painting.

The clouds were painted using various strengths of Payne's Gray/Alizarin Crimson mixes. I wanted some of the cloud edges to be soft and the larger clouds at the top to have harder edges. Timing was important here.

Cadmium Yellow Pale

Raw Sienna

Alizarin Crimson

Payne's Gray

Raw Sienna

Payne's Gray

Cerulean Blue

This cirrus type sky was painted in less than two minutes by applying a very pale Raw Sienna wash to cover the whole of the sky area.

Using broad sweeps of the hake, I painted in the darker Cerulean Blue/Payne's Gray clouds. This type of sky is very easy to paint in less than two minutes.

I could not resist painting this lovely early morning sky. Initially I painted the usual Raw Sienna wash, then added some Alizarin Crimson as I worked downwards.

When the painting was approximately one-third dry, I used a strong Payne's Gray/Alizarin Crimson mix for the cloud formations. A tissue was used to create a few soft white clouds.

Raw Sienna
Payne's Gray
Alizarin Crimson

Raw Sienna
French Ultramarine
Payne's Gray
Alizarin Crimson

Cumulus clouds are like balls of cotton wool floating in the sky. The easiest way to represent them is initially to paint your under-painting using Ultramarine Blue/Payne's Gray mixes, adding darker tones here and there for variation and while still wet, to create the cloud shapes by blotting out using absorbent tissues.

Wet a few of the white clouds at a time with clean water and drop in deeper values of sky colours plus Alizarin Crimson to represent shadows. If it's a sunny day, add a little Raw Sienna to the tops of the clouds to create sparkle.

This soft evening sky was created by initially painting a Cadmium Yellow Pale wash and adding patches of Cerulean Blue, Raw Sienna and Alizarin Crimson. A mixture of Alizarin Crimson and Payne's Gray was used to paint the clouds. The soft edges to the clouds were achieved by painting them when the under-painting was quite wet. It's a matter of timing. Subtlety is what is required here, so don't use garish colours.

Cadmium Yellow Pale
Raw Sienna
Alizarin Crimson
Payne's Gray
Cerulean Blue

PAINTING SKIES *Close up*

This is a fine example of an atmospheric sky. Various techniques were used to create the effect of an approaching storm. The clouds have cast shadows over the land and it's time to seek shelter. There are no bright blues in this sky. The clouds were painted with mixes of Payne's Gray/Cerulean Blue, with a little Alizarin Crimson added to achieve variation, over a wet pale Raw Sienna under-painting. I used a 1½ in hake brush and a minimum of strokes, lightly dancing it across the surface of the 140lb paper.

The whole sky was painted wet into wet in less than three minutes. It's important that the clouds are painted in while the painting is no more than one-third dry, to avoid the occurrence of hard edges (see page 11 for more on this).

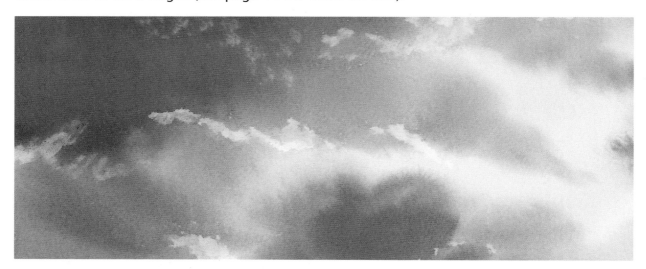

CLOUD FORMATION

The cloud formation, which is probably the most important part of this painting, represents the approaching storm and has therefore been painted in a slightly darker tonal value. The clouds were painted using circular motions with the corner of the hake brush.

The Raw Sienna under-painting was no more than one-third dry when I painted in the clouds, allowing the cloud edges to soften and creating a natural effect. You'll notice that I've separated the cloud formations by leaving a small light area. A simple touch like this can achieve a pleasing effect.

CREATING LIGHT AREAS

To create light areas and realistic cloud formations an absorbent tissue was used to remove colour. A gentle dabbing action was used, turning the tissue to absorb colour and reveal the white of the paper. This technique must be used while the sky area is still wet. It's a simple technique, one I often use to create interesting cloud structures.

DETAILS OF HOUSE

The clouds have not been painted right up to the farmhouse, ensuring counter-change (light against dark, dark against light) between the building and the sky area. This is important, as it makes the buildings and trees behind them stand out against the sky. Note the inclusion of a few sheep and the smoke from the chimney, adding life to the finished painting. The sky shadows have been washed across the foreground.

ADDING INTEREST

The addition of a small splash of another colour can provide a more pleasing sky structure.

You'll notice that I have added a touch of Alizarin Crimson here, to give the picture warmth and variation.

PAINTING SKIES *Project*

Evening Splendour is an ideal painting for the less experienced painter to attempt. It also provides me with the opportunity to introduce you to the concept of glazing. A glaze is produced by mixing a little paint with a lot of water to make a pale-coloured wash.

Glazes can be applied using a traditional watercolour, but an acrylic watercolour has the advantage of allowing several subtle glazes to be applied without the risk of the under-painting lifting.

1. THE SKY AND BUSHES

I positioned masking tape unevenly across the painting to represent the horizon. The sky was painted using a 1½ in hake brush loaded with a weak raw sienna wash, followed by Payne's Gray/Alizarin Crimson mixes for the clouds. Tissues were used to create the cloud shapes.

The bushes were painted using the cloud colours. When these were dry, I applied a little white acrylic to add snow to the foliage which I stippled with a round ended hog-hair brush. When I painted the fence I made sure that the distance between the posts was twice the height of the fence.

2. THE FOREGROUND

The masking tape was slowly removed and the foreground painted by using a stippling action with the hake brush, lightly dancing across the paper to shape the track and represent stubble in the snow. Light sweeps of the hake were applied in the foreground to provide a dry brush effect.

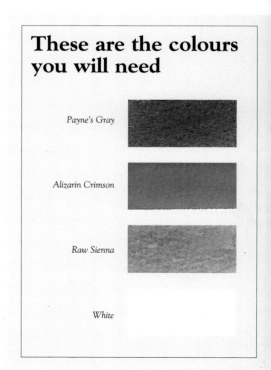

These are the colours you will need

Payne's Gray

Alizarin Crimson

Raw Sienna

White

3. APPLYING THE GLAZE AND ADDING DETAILS

I love snow scenes but they don't have to look cold. I added some warmth to this painting by applying a Raw Sienna glaze over the whole of the sky and adding a little Alizarin Crimson nearer the horizon.

The glaze was mixed in a ceramic saucer and applied with a 1½ in hake brush, working from top to bottom.

I transferred some of the sky glaze to selected areas in the snow to achieve a balance of colour in the painting. When the paint was dry, I felt the addition of a few sheep and a shepherd leaning over the gate would enhance the scene. Detail was added to the track using a rigger brush.

PAINTING SKIES *Project*

1. SKY AND MOUNTAINS

An outline drawing was completed using a dark brown water-soluble crayon. A piece of ³/₄ in masking tape was positioned across the paper to represent the water line. The sky was painted with the usual initial Raw Sienna wash. The clouds were painted using mixtures of French Ultramarine/Payne's Gray. Tissues were used to soften the cloud formations.

The distant mountains were painted with directional strokes of the hake, using a Raw Sienna under-painting. While this was still wet I brushed in various tones of green. An Alizarin Crimson/Payne's Gray mix was used to paint in the far distant mountains. Impressions of trees at the water's edge were painted with a size 6 brush and a few buildings added.

2. MASKING AND FOREGROUND

When dry, the tape was slowly removed. The boat was drawn on a piece of 1¹/₂ in masking tape, cut to shape with a pair of scissors and positioned on the painting to mask the area where the boat was to be placed. The grass areas were painted, working around the right-hand rocky outcrop and a few smaller rocks added.

3. ROCKS AND WATER

The rocky outcrop on the right was painted by applying a Raw Sienna wash and painting in Burnt Sienna and Payne's Gray/Alizarin Crimson mixes. When approximately one-third dry, I used a palette knife to scrape in the rock structures.

The water was painted using the sky colours. I used the side of a size 14 round brush lightly to create sparkle on the water. A few additional rocks were painted on the shore and then the masking tape representing the boat was removed.

4. TREES AND BOATS

I painted in the trees and then the green boat to create interest in the foreground. Using a pre-softened white water-soluble crayon, I added a little sparkle here and there to the rocks.

Finally, the distant fishing boat was simply painted using a rigger brush. Raw Sienna washes were applied to the water to reflect the sky and over parts of the foreground to add warmth to the painting.

These are the colours you will need

Payne's Gray   Alizarin Crimson   Raw Sienna   French Ultramarine   Burnt Sienn

PAINTING SKIES *Using speciality mediums*

Here I want to introduce you to some speciality mediums that I find exciting to use. Do try them where appropriate. You will find them a useful addition to your range of materials.

GRANULATION medium was introduced to provide a granular appearance to colours that normally gave a smooth wash. For maximum effect, if you dilute your colour with medium alone you can achieve a variety of results. I find this medium useful for painting skies or where a light texture effect is required.

PERMANENT MASKING medium is a non-removable transparent liquid mask which can be applied directly to your paper, or mixed with colour and applied to achieve a one-stop mask. It also washes out of brushes very easily by simply rinsing in water; traditional art masking fluid, by contrast, can be difficult to remove from brushes.

Unlike traditional art masking fluid, which has to be applied, dried, painted over, removed and then your element painted in colour, with permanent masking you paint your element in colour, and once it is dry you can over-paint, the masking repelling the wash.

I have used permanent masking to create texture on

In the painting on the right I've used the granulation medium for the sky and permanent masking medium for the tree foliage. For the foliage, I applied the masking with crumpled tissue and over-painted to create the texture.

rocks, foregrounds, foliage etc. Experimenting with this medium has shown me that it works best with light washes. When these are dry, thicker paint can then be applied over the masking to add details.

TEXTURE medium produces a textured finish for watercolours. It can be applied directly to the paper and when dry over-painted or mixed with watercolour and then applied.

LIFTING medium enables the removal of paint at a later stage. Some colours are staining colours and difficult to remove. By applying the lifting medium first, the colour can be easily removed.

BLENDING medium slows drying, providing that extra time sometimes needed when painting in hotter climates. For maximum blending time, dilute your colour with medium alone. Diluting with water will provide a variety of drying times.

In this simple 'doodle' I experimented with a range of mediums.

In the painting on the left I used lifting medium for the sun and over-painted with a Cadmium Yellow wash. When dry, I teased the colour away from the centre by gently rubbing with a small bristle brush and dabbing with a tissue.

To paint the sky, I applied a Cadmium Yellow wash and added some Raw Sienna and Alizarin Crimson as I progressed down to the horizon. The sky colours were transferred into the water. When dry, I added the darker clouds using a mix of Payne's Gray/Alizarin Crimson/Burnt Umber.

Although there is a lot of colour in this sky, it still looks subtle and warm. Don't make your sunsets too bright and overpowering.

Evening Glow *represents a typical evening sky, with the sun going down across the lake.*

The sky was painted by spattering permanent masking, allowing it to dry, then over-painting the sky with blue mixed with granulation medium. The result was the effect of falling snow. Lifting medium was initially painted over the areas filled with fir trees.

I used white paint mixed with texture medium to add the snow to the trees and when this was dry I washed away some colour between the trees. Having previously applied the lifting medium, I was able to lighten these areas. The rocks were formed by using a palette knife.

Ski Patrol *was an experimental painting I completed to test the appropriate use of the speciality mediums.*

PAINTING SKIES *Further techniques*

My aim here is to introduce you to further techniques to enable you to create interesting skies. As the sky can cover two-thirds of your painting, it's important that you practise these techniques to achieve a realistic impression. Glazes can be applied to selected areas in a painting or to the painting as a whole to harmonize the colours, as each colour in the painting will be tinted by the same glaze.

APPLYING A GLAZE

With this scene I applied a warm Raw Sienna wash and added a touch of Alizarin Crimson to selected areas.

Medium tones of Payne's Gray/Alizarin Crimson/Burnt Umber were used to paint the clouds. I used a tissue to create structure in the clouds. When the paint was dry, I mixed a Raw Sienna glaze and, using the hake brush, washed over the whole of the sky area to give it added warmth and glow.

A glaze is a small amount of colour mixed with lots of water.

The glow in the sky was what inspired me to paint **First Snow** with acrylic watercolours. The beauty of acrylics is that if you become bored with a painting, you can apply glazes to change it.

RAIN CLOUDS

Here I applied an initial wet wash of very pale Raw Sienna and quickly painted the dark nimbus clouds with a Payne's Gray/Cerulean Blue mix.

I tilted my watercolour pad until it was almost vertical, allowing the paint to run to represent the shafts of rain. When the paint had run sufficiently, I laid the pad flat and used a tissue to soften the tops of the mountains.

Rain Clouds. *There's not much colour in this study. I painted it as I saw it.*

Evening Light. *You will enjoy this technique. I use it to produce large fresh skies. You must apply strong colours for your over-painting as they will weaken significantly when the paint runs and dries.*

TILTING BOARD

Interesting skies can be painted by applying a wet wash – in this case Raw Sienna – while this is still wet, adding stiffer colours; in this example these were Payne's Gray/Cerulean Blue on the right and Payne's Gray/Alizarin Crimson on the left.

I lifted the board and tilted it in different directions to allow the paint to blend. It takes experience and control to ensure the raw sienna is not completely covered; tilt to the left and, of course, both colours will run to the left, tilt to the right and both will run to the right. When I was happy with the result I laid the board flat again, blotted the sky area with a tissue to add a few white clouds and then allowed the sky to dry naturally.

BRUSHWORK

With this study I painted a weak Raw Sienna wash and, using the hake, brushed in various mixes of Payne's Gray/Cerulean Blue with Alizarin Crimson added to provide variation.

The brush strokes were the important factor in giving the sky the necessary atmosphere. I stroked, dabbed and turned the brush to achieve the desired effect. An absorbent tissue was used to remove paint to represent the patches of white cloud.

The shafts of light were created by applying pressure with a wedge-shaped tissue from the mountain tops upwards.

Winter Majesty *was painted very early on a freezing cold winter's day. The clouds seemed to be moving in several directions, with shafts of light dancing over the mountain tops.*

PAINTING MOUNTAINS *Introduction*

Mountain scenery has always held a great fascination for me. I can't resist painting snow-capped peaks rising upwards to the sky, and even large hills have me reaching for my sketch-pad. This sort of scenery doesn't have to be outside your window for you to paint it: you can do it from a picture you see in a book, magazine, or on television.

Time taken studying the structure of the mountain you are to paint will be well spent. Identify the main features such as distinctive gullies, fissures, promontories and peaks. You'll find a small pair of binoculars invaluable for picking them out. Whatever the characteristics of the mountain you are painting, always simplify its structure. It's not realistic to paint every snow-capped ledge or promontory. Don't forget that you're not trying to reproduce a photograph. Discard any detail that won't significantly contribute to the success of your painting. Concentrate on capturing its profile, its principal structural features,

the variations in colour and tone, the lights and darks. All these considerations will help you to create a believable representation.

Mountains are exciting and challenging to paint. Practise the techniques shown in the following pages and you will soon be able to paint realistic mountains.

You will call on a range of colours to paint mountains. Here are the ones I find most useful:

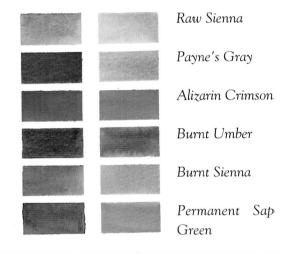

Raw Sienna

Payne's Gray

Alizarin Crimson

Burnt Umber

Burnt Sienna

Permanent Sap Green

Going Fishing *is my vision of a Scottish loch. I used tissues to create the cloud formations and the distant mountain peaks, a palette knife for shaping the rocks, light strokes with the side of a round brush to paint the sparkle on the water, and stippling techniques for the heather and textures in the foreground.*

Check-List

The camera captures a moment in time. The artist expresses his feelings.

- *Don't be too ambitious initially; choose a mountain that you feel lies within your compass of expertise.*
- *Study your subject closely, then simplify its structure, excluding unnecessary details.*
- *Observe the main colours and tones.*
- *Shape your mountain carefully, make it look real.*
- *Don't add details that aren't characteristic of the region you are painting.*

Majestic Peaks *represents the landscape in all its glory and yet also conveys a sense of awe. I have used many techniques here – tissues for the sky, masking in the mountains, the use of a palette knife to create structure and subtle touches of colour to enhance the landscape.*

PAINTING MOUNTAINS *Using colour*

The colours you observe when studying your mountain will vary, depending on the time of day, weather conditions and the season. Changing light or passing clouds will alter the colours and tones. Attempt to retain an image in your mind and paint from that. It is not practical to keep changing your painting as time passes. Also, be aware that the colours become colder and lighter as the mountains recede into the distance.

My usual approach is to shape the mountain using a 1½in wash brush loaded with a weak Raw Sienna. While the paint is still wet I will brush in a variety of colours and tones to form the structure. As the paint dries, I brush in darker tones and shadows until I'm happy that I have created a believable representation.

To achieve the correct balance of colour you will need to experiment with mixing colours. The mixes shown right are just some of the variations possible using the colours shown below left.

The colours shown below right are mixes for mountain peaks and shadows, trees, grass, and varying strengths of Burnt Sienna for under-painting.

	Strong colour	Water added
Raw Sienna		
Payne's Gray		
Alizarin Crimson		
Burnt Umber		
Burnt Sienna		
Permanent Sap Green		

Top row: Payne's Gray and Alizarin Crimson – mountain peaks and shadows
Second row: Burnt Sienna – varying strengths for under-painting
Third row: Payne's Gray and Sap Green – trees
Fourth row: Permanent Sap Green and Raw Sienna – grass areas

BRUSH AND COLOUR EXERCISE

I encourage all my students to experiment with using a flat brush to apply paint.

Try it for yourself – you'll find the brush very versatile and capable of producing a wide variety of marks.

For this project I used a ¾in flat (Winsor & Newton Sceptre Gold II) and four colours (Payne's Gray, Alizarin Crimson, Raw Sienna and Permanent Sap Green). The flat brush is ideal for working around the peaks of the mountain as well as putting in the structure. I hold it at right angles to the paper, approximately 2in above the ferrule.

I took care to leave lots of white paper uncovered, to represent the snow. Mixes of Payne's Gray/Alizarin Crimson were also used.

The directional strokes used for the sky are in a Payne's Gray/Alizarin Crimson mix over a Raw Sienna wash.

The fir trees on the left were painted by adding Permanent Sap Green to the Payne's Gray/Alizarin Crimson mix and applying it with a rocking action to get a stippling effect. The trees in the distance were painted by applying the paint with a dabbing action.

Photography

If you are simply making a sketch as a basis for a painting you will do at home, it can be useful to photograph the scene and use the print as reference.

31

PAINTING MOUNTAINS *Techniques: Creating structures*

Numerous techniques can be used to create mountain structures and features effectively. I find that the structure of the mountain will determine the techniques I use to paint it. In the next few pages I'll show you a variety of techniques that I use.

BRUSHWORK

In **Peace and Tranquillity**, the soft realistic effect is achieved by initially painting a Raw Sienna wash and brushing in darker tones of various colours. Your brush strokes must follow the structure of the mountain. While the paint is still wet I use a damp size 6 brush to create structure.

TRADITIONAL MASKING FLUID

For **Room at the Top**, traditional masking fluid has been applied using a piece of grease-proof paper (plastic wrap or tissue are also worth trying). The grease-proof paper can be pressed to a rough shape for the larger areas or to a point for detail. I often use a cocktail stick dipped in masking fluid to give thin lines.

Once the masking is dry, washes can be applied. I find gentle rubbing with a putty eraser the easiest way to remove the masking.

USING A PAPER WEDGE

In **Pastures New**, I have painted the mountains using various colours and tones and created structure by removing some of the paint while it is still wet. This is done by making a tight wedge of tissue and wiping downwards from the top of the mountain. You'll need to continually form new wedges to ensure the paper does not become stained as the removed paint builds up on the tissue.

If you use this method, ensure that you follow the shape of the promontories of the mountain, otherwise your painting will not look realistic.

PALETTE KNIFE

Where Eagles Fly is a good example of how a palette knife can be used effectively to create texture. I applied a wash of Raw Sienna and brushed in Burnt Sienna and Payne's Gray/Alizarin Crimson mixes. When the paint was no more than one-third dry, the texture was created by moving paint around with the palette knife.

On the next spread we'll look in more detail at other effects that can be achieved with the painting knife.

As we have already seen, the brush is not the only means by which you can achieve realistic effects in your painting. Indeed in some instances you will find the knife is better able to give you the effect you are after.

Most artists are familiar with the use of a knife for oil painting, where it is used to pick up paint and apply it to the canvas. The method of working when using the knife for watercolour painting is somewhat different but very simple.

First, I paint the shapes with a traditional brush. If you apply the knife when the watercolour wash is very wet, the paint is easily moved and the white of the paper is restored. A pleasing dark shadow will result at the base of each stroke.

All types of stonework – such as buildings, mountains, stone walls, cliffs and rocks – can be quickly and realistically painted by applying several colour washes, and when approximately one-third dry applying the knife to create specific effects. Experimenting with different drying times will enable you to achieve a variety of tonal values. This can be particularly useful when you are painting features such as rocks.

*This scene, which I call **Wild Water**, was painted with a knife. Short strokes were used to form the mountains in the distance, while sweeping strokes were required for the boulders in the middle distance and foreground.*

Working with a knife

The effects that can be achieved with the knife are not so effectively produced with a brush.

CLIFFS AND ROCKS

The tip of the knife can be used to create thin lines and the side of the knife to create rocks, promontories or cliffs of different sizes.

I often paint darker shadows underneath foreground rocks to create recession in the painting, as in this example. I used Raw Sienna for the under-painting. Burnt Sienna and a Payne's Gray/Alizarin Crimson mix provided the darker tones.

TEXTURED ROCK SURFACES

This kind of effect is easily achieved and can be used in a variety of situations – for example, to represent a river bank or perhaps the slightly raised surface at the top of a waterfall where the rocks may only protrude a few inches. The shadows can be painted in darker tones.

The effect in the top painting was achieved simply by means of a palette knife. A different kind of texture can be achieved with permanent masking fluid, as seen in the painting below.

This group of rocks was painted by initially applying permanent masking fluid with a little Raw Sienna and when dry, over-painting this with various washes. The permanent masking repels the watercolour to create a textured effect. Unlike traditional masking fluid (see page 30), permanent masking fluid is left on the paper.

PAINTING MOUNTAINS *Close up*

To establish the best vantage point for your composition, complete a quick tonal sketch using a dark brown water-soluble crayon, then compare it with the shape, structure and tonal variations of the scene in front of you.

You can continue modifying the sketch until you're happy that you've achieved an acceptable representation. You'll find this exercise very helpful when you come to apply paint to paper. The beauty of the crayon is that any marks wash out as the painting progresses.

The most time-consuming part of this painting was drawing the outline with the dark brown water-soluble crayon and applying the masking fluid. The drawing and masking were done prior to the sky being painted.

SKY AND WATER

I felt I needed an atmospheric but not too overpowering sky for this painting, because there was lots of detail in the structure of the mountain range. I applied a very weak Raw Sienna wash to wet the paper and brushed in mixes of Payne's Gray/Cerulean Blue/Indanthrene Blue with the 1½ in washbrush (hake). Patches of white cloud were created by using an absorbent tissue to remove the paint.

The colours for the sky were also echoed in the water of the lake. For this, I used the side of a size 14 round brush, taking care to ensure the brush strokes were perfectly level. A light touch of the brush left some of the white paper showing through, representing sparkle on the water. Think of the texture of your paper as representing mountains and valleys. If you move your brush quickly and lightly across the paper you will deposit paint on the peaks of the paper only, leaving the valleys (the white of the paper) uncovered.

TREES

The fir trees were painted using a technique I developed many years ago. I position a piece of ¾in masking tape on the paper to represent the base of the trees, then I take a size 6 rigger brush loaded with paint (in this case Permanent Sap Green), hold it out in front of me, with my hand almost flat to the paper, and dab away at the paper. The shape of the brush ensures that distant trees look realistic. The rock was included to help balance the painting.

Think simple

I produced this painting – **Wilderness** *– from my imagination after reading a series of books by a wonderful American author, David Thompson. It might look complex, but it's really quite simple. Think of it as a jigsaw with each part of the painting representing a piece of the jigsaw. For example, the mountain range can be broken down into several pieces, each one painted separately.*

MOUNTAINS

Once the sky was painted, Raw Sienna and Raw Sienna/Burnt Sienna washes were applied to create light and dark areas in the mountains. A Payne's Gray/Alizarin Crimson mix was added to paint the shadows in the mountains. Never use black for shadows; it kills a painting.

Once dry, remove the masking using a putty eraser and add a Cerulean Blue wash to selected areas of the snow, to represent cloud shadows.

PAINTING MOUNTAINS *Project*

My students enjoy painting **Walk on the Beach**, a coastal scene at evening. The techniques used to paint the cliffs and the rocks on the beach are exactly the same ones I would use for painting mountains.

No initial drawing was done for this project. Instead I positioned a piece of ¾in masking tape horizontally, approximately one third up the painting. The top of the masking tape represents the horizon or water-line.

1. THE SKY

I began with the sky, applying a Raw Sienna wash and, while this was still wet, brushing in Cerulean Blue and splashes of Alizarin Crimson. When the shine had gone off the surface and the wash was approximately one-third dry, the clouds were painted with a Payne's Gray/Alizarin Crimson mix.

Finally, I removed paint with an absorbent tissue to represent cloud structures. The sky was allowed to dry completely.

2. CLIFFS AND ROCKS

The next stage is to paint the distant cliffs in a light tone to achieve recession, darker tones being added as the cliffs become closer. For these, I used a Raw Sienna under-painting with splashes of Burnt Sienna and a Payne's Gray/Alizarin Crimson mix.

When the paint was one-third dry I used a palette knife to move the paint to create the rocky appearance. The paint was dried using a hairdryer and then the masking tape slowly removed.

The same process was used to complete the cliffs on the right of the painting, adding darker tones to the nearest rock grouping.

A smaller, darker group of rocks was added on the left to balance the painting. It always amazes me how realistic-looking rocks can be created: simply by brushing on three colours and moving them around with a palette knife (see page 33).

The sea was painted using a 1½in wash brush loaded with a soft blue mix. To create the effect of distant waves, I moved the brush in horizontal lines, depositing paint every 1½ inches (the width of the brush).

These are the colours you will need

Payne's Gray	Cerulean Blue
Alizarin Crimson	Raw Sienna
Burnt Sienna	

3. THE BEACH AND ADDING THE FIGURES

The beach was painted using horizontal strokes with a 1½ in hake brush. The same colours as for the sky were applied – lighter colours in the distance, darker ones in the foreground. Once dry, the figures were added. Don't forget to add shadows under the figures. I even scratched in a few footprints with the palette knife for realism.

PAINTING MOUNTAINS *Tonal values*

All successful artists appreciate the importance of establishing the lights and darks in their paintings, arranged in relationships that enhance the quality of their work. All paintings need these contrasts, and I don't believe it's possible to produce a good landscape without the careful distribution of tonal values.

It's a common misconception to think that painting is principally about splashing paint on. It's not. When I look at my students' work, in eight cases out of ten I find their paintings lack depth. This is because they don't give enough thought to tonal values. Before you start a painting, I recommend you always produce a simple tonal study to clarify your thinking.

A tonal study is a simple sketch produced in a few minutes to establish the lights and darks in a painting. I complete these to a size of about 3 x 4½ inches using a dark brown water-soluble crayon.

You can find out whether you have passed the tonal values test by taking a black and white photocopy of your completed full colour painting and comparing it with the original. If the tones appear to be the same all over, you'll know you haven't passed it.

In order to achieve recession in this painting of a Scottish loch it was important to paint the distant mountains lighter in tone.

EXERCISES

1. Practise using masking fluid to create snow-capped mountains. Apply the fluid with the use of crumpled grease-proof paper. Use slivers of card dipped in masking for thin lines, cutting off the end after each application to ensure you maintain the thinness. This saves cleaning the brushes.

2. Experiment with a painting knife – you will be amazed at what you can achieve.

3. Practise applying a wash. While the wash is still wet, drop in other colours, allow them to fuse together and move the paint about with a damp brush to create the effect you're looking for.

How to transfer an outline drawing of a completed painting onto watercolour paper

The next technique is not a substitute for learning to draw and should only be used until you are competent at drawing.

1. Take a black and white photocopy of the painting to the size required.

2. Using a soft pencil (6B), scribble across the back of the photocopy.

3. Position the photocopy over your watercolour paper, trace around the outline and key features using a biro or 2H pencil.

4. Remove the photocopy. The image will have transferred to your paper ready for you to apply paint.

In this painting, called **Sunburst**, I applied masking to the mountains and allowed it to dry completely. I painted a circle of Raw Sienna in the sky area and poured pre-mixed washes onto it – Cerulean Blue on the left and Cerulean Blue/Alizarin Crimson on the right. I angled the paper until it was almost vertical and then tilted it to encourage the colours to run together, flow down over the mountains and run off the bottom edge of the paper. I painted darker tones into selected areas in the mountains. Finally the paper was laid flat and allowed to dry completely. The masking was removed to reveal the white of the paper, representing snow on the mountains.

PAINTING LAKE SCENES *Introduction*

Water lends itself ideally to watercolour techniques. Water comes in three types: motionless, as in a puddle in a country lane, a still pond or a calm lake; moving water, as in a slow-moving river, a wind blown lake or a harbour; and turbulent, such as a waterfall, seascape or fast-flowing river.

In this section we will be concentrating on painting lake scenes. Water itself has no colour, it reflects elements around it such as a mountain range, a building or tree, but in the main it is the colours of the sky, a blue, grey, or brown cloud formation that gives the water its colour. A sunset reflected is a beautiful sight.

When you observe a still lake, the rocks, trees, banks and other surrounding objects reflect as a mirror image. It only takes a slight breeze to ruffle the water and the colours change significantly.

You will call upon various colours to paint lakes. Below right are the ones I find most useful.

When painting lakes always bear in mind the following points:
• *Water and reflections are continually shifting, depending on the weather. Don't try to change your painting as the conditions change. Form an initial impression in your mind and paint from that.*
• *Water has no colour; its surface reflects sky and objects around it.*
• *Use the largest brushes possible and apply horizontal brush strokes – water doesn't flow uphill.*
• *Reflections are best painted wet into wet, so paint your water in last, once the reflecting objects have been painted.*
• *Light objects usually reflect darker, dark objects lighter.*
• *To achieve recession in a painting, paint the water lighter in tone near the horizon and darker as it approaches the foreground.*
• *Don't confuse reflections with shadows. Reflections will always be a near vertical mirror image of the reflecting object. The direction of the shadows will depend on the source of light.*
• *The angle of a reflecting object will be opposite in angle to the reflecting object. A tree trunk at an angle is a good example. The reflection will be vertically below the tree but reflected in the water at the opposite angle.*

French Ultramarine

Payne's Gray

Alizarin Crimson

Burnt Umber

Cerulean Blue

In **Snow Capped** *the sky colours were reflected in the water. Sparkle on the water was achieved by moving the brush lightly and quickly across the paper. The atmospheric sky is a feature in this sketch. The foreground rocks were created with a palette knife.*

To paint water that looks real, the secret is to use the minimum number of brush strokes.

Autumn on the Loch. *The reflections were painted as a mirror image of the mountains, using downward strokes with a loaded ³/₄in flat brush. A white water-soluble crayon softened in water was used to indicate wind lines across the loch.*

Basic considerations when painting a lake scene

In the distance you will see a white or pale-coloured line where the light shimmers across the water as it meets the land. Water in a lake is always level, so it's important that your brush strokes take this into account. I have seen so many amateur paintings where the brush strokes haven't been horizontal, giving the impression of the water running downhill.

Recession: This is accomplished by painting distant objects in pale tones and foreground objects in darker tones.

Reflections: For best results use downward strokes with a flat brush, following a mirror image of the reflecting object. Note that the mirror image must be measured from the base of the reflecting object, which may not come down to the water's edge.

43

PAINTING LAKE SCENES *Using colour*

It's not a good idea to have too many colours, because you'll only end up totally confused as to which ones to use. Problems in colour mixing usually result from using a paint box full of tiny pans of colour. If you've got a multitude of pans, they soon become dirty and muddy and frustration quickly follows.

A modest selection of eight colours, plus any special colours you feel you need, is sensible. I prefer tube to pan colours because I like to start each painting with soft, fresh colour. I also like to use a large mixing area which allows me to maintain more space between colours. I always lay the tube colours out in a logical sequence – sky colours, earth colours, mixers.

I mainly use two colour mixes for painting water: Payne's Gray/Cerulean Blue; Payne's Gray/French Ultramarine. I often add a little Alizarin Crimson to brighten the colour mix or a little Burnt Umber to darken the mix. You will produce a wide range of shadow colours if you add 20 per cent of any colour on your palette to 80 per cent Payne's Gray. Don't use black for shadows – it deadens a painting.

To achieve the correct balance of colour you will need to experiment with mixing colours. The mixes shown right are just some of the variations possible using the colours shown below left.

The colours shown below right are mixes for water.

French Ultramarine

Payne's Gray

Alizarin Crimson

Burnt Umber

Cerulean Blue

Strong colour   Water added

Top row: Payne's Gray and Cerulean Blue – surface water
Second row: Payne's Gray and French Ultramarine – surface water
Third row: Payne's Gray and Alizarin Crimson – for pale shadows
Fourth row: Payne's Gray and Burnt Umber – for dark shadows

BRUSHWORK

Let's now concentrate on the actual brushwork used to paint water. I want you to think of your paper texture as mountains and valleys. If you move a loaded brush slowly across the paper, the paint will cover the peaks and run down into the valleys, creating a solid mass of colour we know as a wash. If we move the brush quickly across the paper with a light touch the paint will be deposited on the peaks only and will not have time to run down into the valleys. The result will be broken colour representing sparkle on the water.

PROJECTS

1. Purchase a small watercolour pad and practise your colour mixing.
2. Paint a tree above the river bank and practise wet into wet reflections.
3. Practise creating sparkle on the water by moving the brush quickly across the surface of the paper using a light touch at the end of your strokes.
4. Practise mixing a range of shadow colours by mixing 20 per cent of any colour on your palette with 80 per cent Payne's Gray and adding various amounts of water to create lighter tones.

In this evening sketch, notice how the sky colours are reflected in the water.

Tonal balance

It is a good idea when painting water to use similar colours and tones as those used for the sky. This provides a nice tonal balance for the painting.

PAINTING LAKE SCENES *Project*

Grand Teton National Park in Wyoming offers a breath-taking range of jagged peaks which appear to rise out of Jackson Lake to heights above 13,000 feet. The area is noted for its intense blue skies and these contrast sharply with the snow-capped peaks. The reflection of the mountains in the clear water of Jackson Lake is the subject of this stage-by-stage project, which I've called **Evening in the Tetons**.

1. THE OUTLINE DRAWING AND THE SKY

I positioned ¾ in masking tape across the paper approximately one-third of the way up the painting to represent the water-line. The profile of the mountains was drawn using a dark brown water-soluble crayon.

I used a mixture of French Ultramarine/Payne's Gray, applied with a 1½ in wash brush (hake) to paint the sky. Subtle touches of Alizarin Crimson were added to selected areas. A soft absorbent tissue folded to a wedge shape was used to remove colour by dabbing the paper, to create the white clouds.

2. THE MOUNTAINS

The basic structure of the mountain was painted with a pale wash of Payne's Gray with darker tones applied to the peaks and selected areas. The white of the paper was left uncovered to represent the snow. While the paint was still wet, I used a tissue shaped to a wedge to soften the edges. A size 6 round brush was used to add detail.

Various mixtures of Payne's Gray/Burnt Umber/Permanent Sap Green and Payne's Gray/Alizarin Crimson were used to apply directional strokes with the side of a size 14 round brush upwards from the tape.

I finished by adding a few fir trees at the water's edge, using the size 6 brush loaded with Permanent Sap Green. The masking tape was carefully removed.

3. THE WATER

We now come to the painting of the water. Initially I used a 1½ in wash brush loaded with the sky colours. I kept my brush strokes precisely horizontal to ensure that the water looked level.

When the paint was one-third dry I painted the reflections, using downward strokes with a 1in flat brush. I used the colours of the sky to paint the mountains, ensuring that the reflections were a mirror image of the mountain range. I used a tissue to remove paint to indicate reflections from the snow.

4. ADDING DETAILS AND FINISHING TOUCHES

Using a ¾ in flat brush, I balanced the painting by adding the land area and fir trees (Permanent Sap Green/Payne's Gray mix), and positioning a few rocks.

To finish the painting, I dipped a white water-soluble crayon in water and allowed it to soften before applying it to the fir trees and to the tops of the rocks in the foreground, to represent snow. I applied a few upward strokes of the softened crayon to the surface of the lake, too, to add sparkle to the reflections. Horizontal strokes with the crayon represented wind lines on the surface of the water.

To complete the water, I painted the right-hand side with a little weak Alizarin Crimson to represent reflections from the sky.

These are the colours you will need

Payne's Gray

Alizarin Crimson

Permanent Sap Green

French Ultramarine

Burnt Umber

SKIES, MOUNTAINS and LAKES *Practice*

In this final spread I want you to practise the three principal elements that are the subjects of this book in one watercolour painting: skies, mountains and lakes. The scene I have chosen for this exercise is typical of the Scottish highlands, with a tranquil loch overlooked by a traditional croft, a majestic mountain in the background and a spread of sparkling water. The principal design considerations in this painting are the need for recession and the importance of balance between the elements.

As always, build up your painting. Begin by preparing an outline drawing, then position a piece of masking tape across the paper to represent the horizon or water level. Now, follow my instructions to complete the painting.

THE SKY

As we have seen, the sky establishes atmosphere and mood, and takes up almost two-thirds of a painting. A fresh wet into wet sky is required here, with cool darker clouds painted in on the left to balance the warm colours of the croft. The mixture for the cloud structures was produced with Payne's Gray and the addition of a little Cerulean Blue and Alizarin Crimson over a Raw Sienna under-painting. A soft absorbent tissue was used to remove some of the colour to shape the cloud formations and soften their edges.

THE MOUNTAINS

For the sake of realism it is important that your brush strokes follow the structure of the mountain. After initially applying a Raw Sienna wash, I used a Payne's Gray/Cerulean Blue mix for the peaks of the mountains in the foreground. Then I used a tissue pressed to a wedge (see page 30 for technique) to remove paint and create the features of the mountains.

A Permanent Sap Green/Payne's Gray mixture applied with a dabbing action was used for the impression of trees at the foot of the mountains.

To achieve recession, the distant mountain was painted in light tones of a mixture of Payne's Gray/Alizarin Crimson. Then I used a tissue to soften the structure, enhancing the illusion of recession.

THE LAKE

In order to create sparkle on the water, move your loaded brush quickly and lightly across the surface of the paper. This will leave some of the white of the paper uncovered to represent light on the water. The boat is important compositionally and was added to balance the building diagonally.

The colours used were a mixture of Payne's Gray/Cerulean Blue/Alizarin Crimson. When these were dry, I applied a pale wash of Raw Sienna to selected areas.

BUILDINGS AND FOREGROUND

The roof of the croft adds warmth to the painting. It was painted with a mixture of 20 per cent Alizarin Crimson and 80 per cent Burnt Sienna. The smoke was achieved by painting a little white over a Payne's Gray under-painting.

The foreground was painted by applying several washes of green made from mixes of Permanent Sap Green and Raw Sienna. Payne's Gray was added to the mixture to darken the green in the near foreground.

The rocks and stone wall were added using mixes of Raw Sienna and Burnt Umber. While the paint was still wet, a tissue was used to remove paint from the tops of the rocks to represent light reflecting off them.

Levelling the water-line

When painting mountains that fall down to the water's edge, I position a piece of masking tape across the paper, representing the water line and paint my mountains down to the tape. If the paint goes over the tape slightly, it doesn't matter. When the paint is dry, I carefully remove the tape. The water-line will appear perfectly level – a useful technique.

49

TREES, ROCKS & RUNNING WATER

PAINTING TREES *Introduction*

A tree is a living organism that reflects the warmth of spring by growing fresh shoots and leaves. In the autumn it slows down its growth and in many species assumes marvellous autumn tints before shedding its leaves. The evergreens, of course, retain their foliage, providing contrast with their bare deciduous cousins. Each tree displays its own character through its shape.

I spent my childhood playing in acres of mixed woodland. I imagine that's why I love trees and enjoy painting them. You don't have to know the name of a tree in order to paint it successfully, but being able to paint trees that look like trees requires an understanding of basic shape and structure. We'll be looking at these in more detail later.

I get a great deal of enjoyment just from looking at trees. Certainly, careful observation will help you to get your painting of them right. When I'm painting trees I take the following points into consideration:

- Does the structure of the tree look sufficiently sturdy to support its foliage?
- Does the base of the trunk look as if it is capable of supporting the boughs, which support the branches, which support the twigs – each becoming thinner as they reach out from the trunk?
- What is the arrangement of the branches on the boughs? In nature branches rarely grow opposite each other on a bough. Make sure you reflect this in your painting.

The way the brush is used and the fluidity of the paint is most important. In the following pages I aim to show you a wide range of techniques for painting trees and bushes.

The colours I find most useful are shown below.

Winter's Flow *shows the importance of a soft atmospheric background to the bare tree structures, which were scratched out with a palette knife. Darker tones were painted on the trunks of the trees to represent texture.*

Payne's Gray

Permanent Sap Green

Cerulean Blue

Cadmium Yellow Pale

Raw Sienna

Burnt Sienna

Burnt Umber

Alizarin Crimson

First Catch *was painted in acrylic watercolours. Pale tones were used to represent the distant trees and a variety of tonal values and colours went into painting the groups of trees. It was important to give a rough texture to the bank in the foreground. The red/Sienna roof of the old building contrasts nicely with the green of the trees.*

Points to remember

- If your tree is going to look as though it's growing, it's important to show a diminishing thickness from trunk to bough, and from bough to branch and twig.
- Always leave some gaps in the foliage so that you can paint a few branches showing through. This gives a sense of structure.
- Trees display a variety of tonal values in their foliage.
- Trunks vary in colour between the seasons, from a pale grey to a rich red brown, depending on the particular variety of tree.

- Coniferous trees look the same in summer and autumn – they don't shed their leaves. Deciduous trees shed their leaves and look entirely different when unfrocked.
- Shadows give depth to foliage. Trees look dark on the inside and light on the outside.
- Mature trees weren't planted yesterday, so show some vegetation growing around their base.
- Recession is achieved by painting distant trees with pale cool colours and foreground trees with warm rich colours.

PAINTING TREES *Tree shapes*

Of all the elements in a painting, it's the painting of trees that my students find most difficult. Trees need to be represented convincingly. You don't have to paint them as botanical specimens but as impressions. Structure, tone and colours are what you're going to have to master. Trees can be simplified for painting purposes into three basic shapes: the pyramid, the upturned bucket and the upturned teacup. We'll look at each of these in turn.

Pale washes initially establish the shape of the tree. Darker tonal mixes are added to paint the detail and add depth to the foliage.

PYRAMID
Examples include:
conifer, spruce,
Lombardy poplar,
fir and pine.

To paint this Norwegian spruce I used a ¾ in one stroke brush with an initial pale tone of a Permanent Sap Green/Payne's Gray mix followed by darker tones of the same mix to create depth.

UPTURNED BUCKET
Examples include:
beech, oak, elm,
chestnut, poplar
and ash.

To paint this tree I used a size 14 round brush with the brush held as flat to the paper as possible and the handle virtually horizontal. Short downward strokes, lightly touching the paper, are required.

UPTURNED TEACUP
Examples include:
weeping willow,
gorse and bushes in
hedgerow.

This weeping willow has been painted using identical downward strokes as described above. The shape is very similar but more of a semi-circle.

DESIGN CONSIDERATIONS – EXERCISES

● *Build your understanding of structure by sketching trees when the leaves have fallen.*

● *Choose different tree types – deciduous and evergreen – and paint the same tree in each of the seasons. You will be amazed at the changes you observe.*

● *Practise painting the same tree at different times of the day: early morning, midday and evening. You'll notice significant variations as the light changes. Paint the shadows.*

Winter Light, *an acrylic watercolour demonstration to an art society, shows how recession is achieved by painting distant trees wet into wet with minimal detail and painting trees and bushes in the foreground in greater detail.*

Aerial perspective

Trees in the distance should be painted in lighter tones with cooler colours and in less detail. Add warmer and richer colours to trees in the middle distance and foreground. Also include some detailed tree structure. This approach helps the viewer look into the painting.

PAINTING TREES *Colour mixing*

In this section, I want you to practise mixing a wide variety of colours to give you greens and autumn tints for painting foliage. You can also create lovely greys, which will add depth to the trees and bushes you paint. Over 100 shades of green can be produced by mixing combinations of the colours below.

To achieve the correct balance of colour you will need to experiment with mixing colours. The mixes shown here are just some of the variations possible using the colours shown below.

The colours shown opposite are mixes useful for trees at different times of the year.

Strong colour	Water added		Strong colour	Water added	
		Payne's Gray			Raw Sienna
		Permanent Sap Green			Burnt Sienna
		Cerulean Blue			Burnt Umber
		Cadmium Yellow Pale			Alizarin Crimson

MIXING COLOURS

Practise mixing the following combinations of colours. The quantity of water you use will, of course, determine the depth of the colours.

Soften your greens by adding Raw Sienna or darken them by adding Payne's Gray, Alizarin Crimson, Burnt Umber or Burnt Sienna.

GREENS
Payne's Gray and
Permanent Sap Green

Permanent Sap Green and
Raw Sienna

Cerulean Blue and
Cadmium Yellow Pale

Cerulean Blue and
Raw Sienna

AUTUMN COLOURS
Burnt Sienna and
Raw Sienna

Alizarin Crimson and
Raw Sienna

Alizarin Crimson and
Cadmium Yellow Pale

GREYS
Payne's Gray and
Permanent Sap Green

Payne's Gray and
Cerulean Blue

Payne's Gray and
Alizarin Crimson

PAINTING TREES *Creating realistic foliage*

The inexperienced landscape painter finds great difficulty in representing the foliage on trees and bushes realistically. Here are five simple techniques for you to practise.

To create this loosely painted group of bushes, I initially loaded a size 14 round brush with pale Raw Sienna and holding it close to the paper, with the brush almost horizontal, I applied a series of quick downward strokes following the shape of the bushes, lightly depositing paint on the paper – see demonstration opposite.

While the paint was still wet I repeated the process, this time with stiffer mixes of mid to dark green colours to give variation and depth to the bushes. I used my thumb-nail to scratch in some structure.

This group of trees and bushes in a hedgerow was painted using an oil painter's round hog-hair brush – see demonstration opposite. Several colours and tones were painted using a stippling action to create a more detailed representation. I used my thumbnail to scratch in some structure; a cocktail stick or corner of a palette knife could be used instead.

This 'doodle' illustrates the effect of recession. To achieve recession, I painted the distant trees in cool colours, using the quick downward strokes described in the first example. The grouping in the foreground was then painted. To add the necessary detail to this grouping, I used a stippling action. You could try using a piece of crumpled tissue or grease-proof paper dipped in paint or a natural sponge to achieve this – see demonstration opposite. Test the effect on scrap paper first.

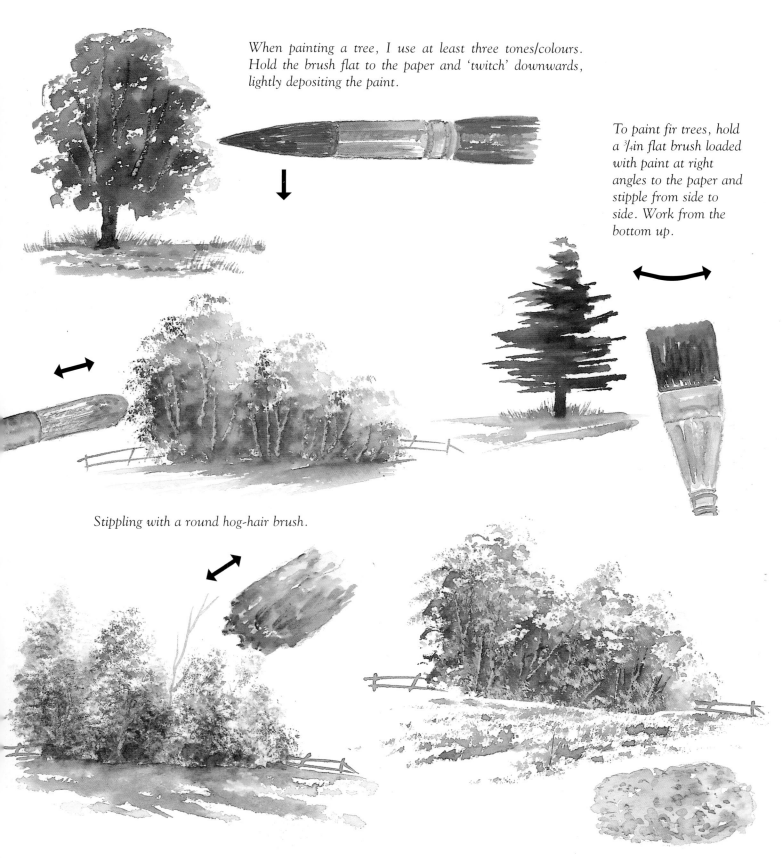

When painting a tree, I use at least three tones/colours. Hold the brush flat to the paper and 'twitch' downwards, lightly depositing the paint.

To paint fir trees, hold a ³/₄in flat brush loaded with paint at right angles to the paper and stipple from side to side. Work from the bottom up.

Stippling with a round hog-hair brush.

Stippling with a crumpled piece of grease-proof paper.

Using a sponge to create texture. Don't squeeze the sponge as you stipple.

PAINTING TREES *Close up*

I never complete a painting in one sitting. I prefer to look at it over a two-week period so I can make any changes I feel are necessary.

These changes may involve removing paint, or adding highlights or more detail. In **Autumn Gold** I added depth to the foliage of the trees in the right foreground, to help balance the painting.

Before I began this painting, I positioned a piece of ³/₄in wide masking tape a third of the way up the paper, the top of the tape representing the distant water-line.

THE TREES

First, I used a sliver of mounting card dipped in masking fluid to draw in the main shapes. For the fine lines, I used a cocktail stick dipped in the masking. The next stage was to mask the tree foliage. The technique I used was to crumple a piece of grease-proof paper, dip it in the masking fluid and stipple in the shapes of the foliage. (Crumpled tissue or plastic wrap can also be used. Which you choose will depend on the size of the deposits you wish to make.)

Once the masking was dry, I brushed in washes of pale green, Raw Sienna and Payne's Gray/Alizarin Crimson, tilting my board to allow the colours to blend.

I removed the masking when the washes had dried. I brushed pale washes of the colours into the white areas to make the foliage of the trees look realistic. Some detail was painted into the tree structures using a rigger brush. When this had been done, I carefully removed the masking tape.

THE ROCKS

The rocks are an important feature in this painting. I drew them with a paint brush dipped in Raw Sienna in order to establish the shapes. When the paint was one-third dry I took a size 6 brush and added Burnt Sienna and Alizarin Crimson mixed with Payne's Gray. I moved the paint around to create structure. When I needed to remove surplus colour, I used a paper tissue shaped to a point.

THE WATER

Masking fluid was applied to the areas between the rocks, where the fast-flowing water was to be painted, and to other areas of white water. When the masking was dry, I used a hake brush to paint the whole of the river area, washing over the masking. When this was dry, the masking was removed.

The hairs of a size 14 round brush loaded with Payne's Gray were spread between thumb and forefinger to fan the hairs to create fine lines. Then I painted the fast-flowing water between the rocks, using quick, light directional strokes of the brush.

PAINTING TREES *Project*

I was asked to paint this **Constable Country** for a TV programme. The challenge was to represent the great variety of trees, bushes and vegetation effectively, given the size of the painting (22in x 15in). I chose to stipple with a sponge, which enabled me to build up the detail and make a pleasing final picture. If I'd chosen unwisely, and opted instead to use a brush, I would have had to apply a great number of brush strokes and the painting could have ended up looking lack-lustre as a consequence.

1. DRAWING AND PREPARATION

I used a water-soluble crayon for the initial drawing. A pale blue wash was applied to paint the sky and when this was dry I painted a rough representation of trees by stippling with a sponge dipped in various tones of green. Washes were applied to the river bank, made by mixing Raw Sienna, Cerulean Blue and Permanent Sap Green. When using the sponge, don't squeeze it or you will create surplus water, resulting in blobs of paint rather than an open effect to represent the foliage effectively.

2. THE FOLIAGE

More detail was added to the trees, using a stippling action with the sponge, and the initial shape of the bushes defined. I used a blue-green for the tree on the left, and added more yellow to produce a softer green for the tree on the right. The colour mixes used for the foliage were made from combinations of Cerulean Blue, Cadmium Yellow Pale, Raw Sienna and Payne's Gray, to darken the mixes to add depth to the foliage. A touch of Alizarin Crimson/Burnt Sienna was used to paint the flowers in the distance. (A technique called negative painting was used in the representation of the chairs on the patio. This is when you paint around the object you wish to preserve.)

‡. ADDING DETAIL

'he roofs of the buildings were painted using a mix of pproximately 20 per cent Burnt Sienna/80 per cent Alizarin Crimson. The tree structures were painted sing Raw Sienna/Burnt Umber mixes. For the trunk, I pplied a Raw Sienna wash and while this was still wet dded darker tones of Burnt Umber.

Now let's bring the painting together. To shape the distant trees and the middle distance bushes, I stippled with a hog-hair brush loaded with mixes of soft green and yellow greens. The reeds were painted on the river bank. Detail and shadows were added. Finally, the water and reflections were painted wet-into-wet and the white fence on the left side was painted using a dry white water-soluble crayon.

These are the colours you will need

| Payne's Gray | Cerulean Blue | Alizarin Crimson | Raw Sienna | Burnt Umber | Cadmium Yellow | Permanent Sap Green | Burnt Sienna |

PAINTING TREES *Project*

Successful artists continually try new ways of capturing the landscape in paint. They experiment with new methods, try new tools and look at their work critically. Some of their new practices will be successful, others will fail. Either way they will learn and through their endeavours extend the range of techniques available to them when painting a landscape.

I have painted the scenery shown in **First Snow** in all seasons, in this case in autumn. The light covering of snow contrasts with the colours of the autumnal foliage. I used a number of unconventional techniques in this painting, as you will see.

1. DRAWING, MASKING, POURING PAINT

I drew the outline of the trees and the river bank with a dark brown water-soluble crayon. Using a piece of crumpled grease-proof paper dipped in masking fluid, I stippled over the trees to create impressions of foliage.

I masked some of the tree structures, using a cocktail stick dipped in masking fluid. I also applied masking to the river banks and light areas in the water, this time by means of an old brush.

Then I mixed several ample washes in saucers. The colours I chose for this were Cadmium Yellow Pale, Cerulean Blue, Payne's Gray/Alizarin Crimson and Permanent Sap Green. After inclining the board at about five degrees, I poured the washes over the paper. Cadmium Yellow Pale was poured first, followed by Cerulean Blue in the centre, then the Payne's Gray/Alizarin Crimson mix, and finally Permanent Sap Green over the trees on the right-hand side of the painting. Burnt Sienna was brushed into the trees on the left side.

While the washes were still wet I tilted the board until it was almost vertical to allow the washes to blend, run down the paper and off the bottom of the board. Sometimes the masking restricted the flow of paint, so I used a round brush to push paint around the masking. An occasional spray of clean water from a spray bottle encouraged the flow of paint. Surplus paint was removed with an absorbent tissue. The board was then laid flat. When the paint was almost dry I used a hairdryer to make sure the paint was completely dry.

2. FURTHER POURING, ADDING DETAIL

Using a size 14 round brush loaded with the Payne's Gray/Alizarin Crimson mix, I added depth to selected areas of the foliage. These darker tones give the foliage depth and structure and achieve recession in the painting.

I added the fir trees by stippling with a ¾in flat brush loaded with Permanent Sap Green. For the distant firs, I added more water to lighten the colour. I used a hair-dryer to dry the paint completely.

3. REMOVING THE MASKING

Using a putty eraser gently, I removed the masking from the trees and river banks. I find the masking adheres to the eraser and comes off the paper cleanly.

4. GLAZING AND PAINTING THE WATER

Washes of Cadmium Yellow Pale, Raw Sienna, Burnt Sienna and Permanent Sap Green were applied to the areas of white paper to add a range of autumn colours to the foliage. Subtle hints of colour used for the foliage were transferred to the river banks. I felt the inclusion of the rocks helped to balance the painting. Finally, I removed the masking from the water.

5. BRINGING THE PAINTING TOGETHER

This is the time to add the final touches. I have included a rock in the foreground to improve the composition, and also darkened the fir trees on the left-hand side with a Payne's Gray/Alizarin Crimson glaze. Using a chisel-ended hog-hair brush dipped in white gouache,

a light dressing of snow was painted on the fir trees and a few bushes along the top of the river banks.

Finally, I softened the end of a white water-soluble crayon in water and then used it lightly to create sparkle in selected areas of the river.

PAINTING TREES *Creating tree structures*

Several techniques can be used to paint tree structures. Some of the most interesting involve the use of a palette knife. In addition to this technique, you will also find advice on how to use permanent masking medium to create structures and how to add interest to an underlying structure.

USING A PALETTE KNIFE

After painting the background, I left the paint until it was approximately one-third dry and then, using a palette knife, moved the paint about to create the tree structures.

You will need to purchase a knife and practise with it before you try this technique in a real painting. The width of the structure of your tree will depend on how you use the knife: press down hard with the whole edge of the knife and you will get a trunk that is the width of your knife; press lightly and you will produce narrower widths; use the corner or edge of the knife and you'll produce thin lines.

USING PERMANENT MASKING MEDIUM

The tree structure here was painted using permanent masking medium. With traditional masking fluid, several stages would be involved. Permanent masking medium is mixed with colour, the subject painted and left on the paper. When dry it will repel light washes.

In stage one the masking medium was applied to create the tree structure. In stage two detail was added to the trunk with the masking medium, and when this was dry a background wash was applied.

CREATING REALISM

In the first stage of this painting I used Raw Sienna for the under-painting, to determine the shape, and while this was still wet overpainted with a deeper green. To add depth to the tree some Payne's Gray was overpainted when the first stage was approximately one-third dry.

Finally the trunk was painted and some branches were scratched in using a palette knife. Realism and depth have been achieved by ensuring that the tree is darker on the inside.

In this painting I used permanent masking medium to paint in the tree structures, the palette knife to scratch out branches and also texture medium to give the foliage texture. The texture medium added to the colour makes the paint thicker and less watery. Note how I have achieved the impression of recession by painting the distant trees in lighter tones.

FOLIAGE AS STRUCTURE

In this example the trunks have been over-painted to represent ivy. This is simply painted by adding a dark under-painting and, when this is dry, taking a hog-hair brush, dipping this in a soft green mixed with a little white gouache or acrylic paint and stippling in impressions of leaves.

Adding tonal value

To ensure your trees look realistic and have depth, it is important to over-paint with darker toned glazes.

PAINTING ROCKS *Techniques*

The painting of rocks has always been a difficult subject for the beginner to master. In a river, they may look rounded or long and flat, as they have been shaped over the years by fast-flowing water. In a mountainous region they may appear pointed or roughly structured where they have been broken off larger deposits and have rolled down to find their own place in the landscape.

Their composition will have contributed to their structure and shape, depending on whether they are of a soft material or a hard brittle volcanic rock. Fortunately, as artists, we only have to paint them to look natural in their environment. The careful positioning of rocks in a painting can significantly improve the composition or balance. Their positioning may be determined by choosing the best vantage point from which to view the scene, or using artistic licence.

Like all subjects there are different ways to paint rocks. I always try to use the most appropriate technique, and this may depend on my mood at the time, or the size, shape or position of the rocks in the landscape.

In this technique, I washed in some Raw Sienna and Burnt Sienna and while this was still wet added darker, stiffer tones of a Payne's Gray/Alizarin Crimson mix to create structure and depth. The paint was allowed to blend into the under-painting.

Here, I've painted an initial Raw Sienna wash and added some Burnt Sienna and darker tones of Payne's Gray/Alizarin Crimson. I used a crumpled piece of absorbent tissue to remove the paint, creating a textured appearance.

These rocks were created by initially painting their structure using a variety of dark tones and, when these were dry, adding highlights with a softened white water-soluble crayon. You can blend the white in, using a damp brush, or colour the rock by adding Burnt or Raw Sienna to the white.

This waterfall is typical of many to be found in the English Lake District in the autumn when the water levels are high. The water is tumbling down from the mountains, washing its way through a rocky landscape.

The rocks were painted with a flat brush, using several tones and colours; I used Raw Sienna, Alizarin Crimson and Payne's Gray, and when they were dry added highlights with a softened white water-soluble crayon.

I was fascinated by the sea pounding the rocks in this sketch, completed on a painting tour of South Africa. To create the effect of the spray, I used a combination of the white of the paper and directional strokes with the side of a softened white water-soluble crayon.

Creating variation

Practise painting a group of rocks, creating variation in your grouping; make the first rock rounded, the second larger and angular, and then place an even larger and pointed rock behind the two.

PAINTING ROCKS *Design considerations – Colour mixing*

- When painting rocks, don't make them all the same size, shape or form. Don't paint them equally spaced.

- When painting rocks in water, don't forget to display shadows or they will look as if they are floating on the water.

- Rocks on land will have some type of vegetation growing around their base.

- Determine the direction of the light and add highlights and shadows.

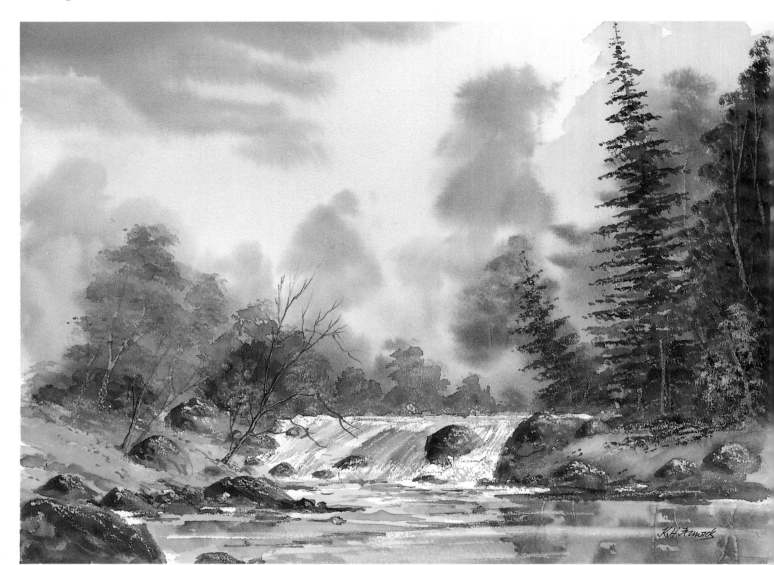

Water Rhapsody *was a waterfall I discovered on one of my walks in the wilds of Scotland. I painted the falling water with a hake brush, using fast strokes and only lightly touching the paper. Note the variation in the size, shape and spacing of the rocks – all principles of good design.*

Exercise: Using the palette knife

Using the palette knife effectively requires practice. Try this simple exercise. Cover with any dark colour an A4 size piece of watercolour paper. When the paint is less than one-third dry, see how many different shapes and effects you can produce with the knife. Now, try painting the simple rock group at the bottom of page 27.

The colour combinations shown below are those I use most often for painting rocks. Using these combinations in conjunction with varying amounts of water, I'm able to produce a wide range of tonal values.

I may also introduce other colours, depending on what I see in front of me. If, for example, the rocks are covered in lichen or moss, I will add some raw sienna or green or whatever colour I feel it is appropriate to use.

Raw Sienna and Burnt Sienna

Payne's Gray and Cerulean Blue

Payne's Gray and Alizarin Crimson

Payne's Gray and Burnt Umber

In this painting, which I call **Windblown** *because of the directional leaning of the trees, I used a palette knife to create the various rocks.*

Initially three washes were applied with the flat brush. While the paint is less than one-third dry, it is easily moved with the palette knife and the white of the paper restored. As can be seen, there is a pleasing dark shadow at the base of each stroke.

These rocks have been created by applying washes. While these were still wet, I moved the paint around with a palette knife. Some detail was added when the paint was dry.

71

PAINTING WATER *Introduction*

Water is a constant source of inspiration for the landscape painter, offering a choice of river scenes, waterfalls, lakes, ponds, seascapes and even puddles in a country lane. As artists we are faced with three types of water:

- Motionless – eg, a calm lake, the local pond, a puddle on a woodland path or even a rain-drenched street scene.
- Moving – eg, rivers, mountain becks, wind-blown lakes.
- Turbulent – eg, a fast-flowing waterfall, mountain beck or stormy seascape.

In this chapter we will concern ourselves with the last two types.

MOVING WATER

In a fast-flowing river or mountain beck, the whiteness of the water provides an indication of the speed of flow, particularly when the flow is restricted by rocks.

Water is best painted using the minimum number of brush strokes and a light touch of the brush. As a general rule, the faster the flow the lighter and quicker your brush strokes should be.

I like to sit by the water and observe the flow patterns, colours, tones, shadows and reflections. Squinting one's eyes to observe the flow helps establish the main characteristics. I like to produce a quick tonal study with a dark brown water-soluble crayon. When it is finished I hold it in front of me and compare it with the actual scene. If I feel changes are necessary, I will sketch them in prior to painting the scene. Too much detail makes water look fussy and unnatural. The key word is 'simplify'.

TURBULENT WATER

There is no more beautiful sight than a tumbling mountain beck or waterfall. The speed of flow and the depth of water will determine whether the water appears light or dark in tone where the water flows over a shelf or rock. When the flow is interrupted by rocks the effect will be of white water.

When turbulent water has completed its fall or been restricted by rocks, some spray may occur. The water will be darker in tone as it flows away from the base of the fall or a rocky outcrop.

I find a camera useful to capture the flow pattern, which sometimes the eye and brain have difficulty in determining.

River Rhapsody *represents fast-flowing water through a rocky river bank.*

Payne's Gray

French Ultramarine

Cerulean Blue

Alizarin Crimson

Burnt Umber

To paint water that looks real, the secret is to use the minimum number of brush strokes.

Reflections *was a painting commissioned by an international construction company. The reflections are mirror images of the reflecting objects and the sky colours repeat on the surface of the water.*

REFLECTIONS

Reflections will appear blurred in moving water, and as a mirror image in still water. Where there are reflecting objects, I paint the water last. A wet wash is painted followed by vertical strokes for the reflections.

It's important to understand that reflections reflect from the base of the reflecting object. For example, a large tree or building a field away may only reflect its top in the water, not its whole.

General guide to painting water

Brush strokes should follow the flow.

Shadows should be painted horizontal.

Reflections should be painted vertical.

To achieve freshness, apply quick brush strokes using a light touch of the brush.

USING TEXTURE
Think of the texture of your paper as being like mountains and valleys. If you move your brush quickly and lightly across the mountain tops, the paint will be deposited on the peaks of the paper, and not be allowed time to run down into the valleys. The result is broken colour. You can use this technique to create sparkle on water – see painting on opposite page.

USING PERMANENT MASKING MEDIUM
Here I have used permanent masking medium to paint the reflections representing the tree structures. I used a cocktail stick dipped in the medium to draw the fine lines; this saves cleaning a brush. When the masking was dry the water and reflections of the trees/bushes were painted over it. The masking repelled the liquid washes. With permanent masking – as the name suggests – you don't remove it.

USING A HAKE BRUSH
This water was painted using a hake brush. It's a good idea to practise first on a piece of paper similar to the paper you are using for your painting. Remember, fast strokes with a light touch are required for painting water. When you have managed to deposit the paint in this manner on your test paper, paint in the water on your landscape.

USING A RIGGER BRUSH
I've used downward strokes with the side of a size 6 rigger (a size 6 round will suffice) to paint the water. Take care, it's so easy to apply too many coats. The aim is to leave lots of white paper showing through. Just a twitch of the brush is required to achieve the light, quick strokes you need to paint water.

CREATING SPARKLE

Here I've demonstrated the technique discussed opposite to create sparkle on the water. The size 14 round brush or the hake should be held as flat to the paper as possible to achieve the desired effect.

CREATING REFLECTIONS

I scratched out the background tree structures and their reflections in the water using my thumbnail when the paint was approximately one-third dry. If this technique is used when the paint is very wet, a black line will result as the scratched out areas fill in with wet paint. Timing is important.

CREATING FALLING WATER

In this simple exercise, the falling water was painted using the side of a rigger brush, with the brush strokes following the angle of flow.

I painted the background trees in cool colours, wet into wet, to achieve recession and scratched out the tree structures. The texture on the rocks was created using a palette knife.

PAINTING WATER *Colour mixing*

Problems in colour mixing usually result from using a palette that isn't large enough for the purpose. You will need a large mixing area that allows you to display the colours with adequate spaces between them. I find it essential to lay out my colours in a logical sequence – sky colours, earth colours and mixers.

I prefer tube colour to the small hard pans of colour because I like to begin each painting with soft fresh colour.

I often add a little Alizarin Crimson to brighten the mix or a little Burnt Umber to darken the mix. For shadows, if you add 20 per cent of any colour on your palette to 80 per cent Payne's Gray you will be able to produce a wide range of interesting greys. Don't use black for shadows – it deadens a painting.

To achieve the correct balance of colour you will need to experiment with mixing colours. The mixes shown here are just some of the variations possible using the colours shown below.

The colours shown opposite are mixes for water.

Payne's Gray

French Ultramarine

Cerulean Blue

Alizarin Grimson

Burnt Umber

Strong colour   *Water added*

Strong colour   *Water added*

76

Water is colourless – its surface displays the colours of the elements reflected in it.

These are the colour mixes I use most for painting water; which mix you use will, of course, depend on where you are painting. Practise mixing them yourself.

Payne's Gray and Cerulean Blue
Surface water

Payne's Gray and French Ultramarine
Surface water

Payne's Gray and Alizarin Crimson
Pale shadows

Payne's Gray and Burnt Umber
Dark shadows

In **Scottish Landscape** I used quick, light strokes with the hake brush to achieve the effect of fast-flowing water.

Hartsop Beck in the Lake District is one of my favourite places to paint. I made a TV programme there and to me it represents the countryside at its best. The main feature of this acrylic painting is the fast-flowing beck, which is fed by water flowing from the mountains, running through the old hamlet of Hartsop.

THE TREES

Let's begin with the tall birch tree just off-centre. Using the rigger brush, I painted its structure in pale Burnt Umber. When the paint was dry, I painted the foliage with the side of a size 14 brush using light downward strokes. The colours I chose were mixes of pale green to Burnt Sienna. When this was dry, darker tones were painted on the tree structure to achieve a more realistic effect.

The tree on the left was darker in tone. I used the same process as described above but in this instance darker tones of Payne's Gray/Permanent Sap Green were added to create depth in the foliage. To achieve a realistic impression of foliage, I stippled with a round-ended hog-hair brush loaded with a pale green.

THE ROCKS

The rocks are a feature in this painting. Various glazes of Raw Sienna, Burnt Sienna and Payne's Gray were applied to create the three dimensional look of the rocks. Acrylics enable several glazes to be applied without the worry of lifting the underpainting.

Using a 'scumbling' action the rigger brush was used to apply a little white paint mixed with raw sienna to create texture and highlights on the rocks. Think of 'scumbling' as pressing the brush to the paper and 'wiggling' it about to deposit paint in various patterns. Finally I used the rigger brush to paint in a few cracks or fissures in the rocks and added a few darker shadows.

Hartsop Beck *– a fine example of fast-flowing water in an area of outstanding natural beauty.*

THE WATER

Initially, I used the side of the rigger brush to paint the flow lines between each of the rocks, representing flowing white water. The next stage was to paint some medium tones as horizontal lines to fill in the expanses of water between each level of rock. For this I used the hake brush. Finally, I added some darker tones to each side of the river bank to represent reflections and give depth to the water.

The colours used to paint the water were Cerulean Blue and Payne's Gray in various mixes and tones. The water area was painted in less than three minutes. In order to achieve recession in this painting, more white of the paper was left uncovered in the distant water.

PAINTING WATER *Tonal values – Design considerations*

An understanding of tonal values is the most important factor in painting a successful landscape. It's important to clarify one's thinking and approach to the painting before contemplating applying paint to paper. Many of my students splash paint on without careful planning and design. A black and white photocopy of one of their paintings will show how far they have got it wrong, as the copy will reveal the same tone throughout.

In this first attempt by one of my students, there's little variation in tonal values between the trees in the foreground and those in the distance. The cloudless sky does little to balance the right-hand tree grouping. The rocks appear as if they are floating on the water and there's no variation in colour. There's insufficient detail to interest the viewer.

This is a more interesting representation than the previous painting because of the tonal variation in the various elements. I painted the clouds on the left darker in tone to balance the more detailed tree grouping on the right, and also added darker values to the trees for depth. Notice too the shadows in the water and under the rocks, and the texture in the foreground. Note that the distant trees have been painted in lighter tones to achieve recession.

So, what should they have done? To begin with, I always produce small tonal sketches of the scene from different vantage points to determine which of them is going to produce the best composition and to establish the lights and darks in the painting.

These sketches are very simple, about 3in x 4½in in size, and produced in a few minutes with a dark brown water-soluble crayon. I can draw with the crayon and then spread the paint with a moist brush.

DON'T ALWAYS PAINT WHAT YOU SEE

My students always look puzzled when I explain to them why they shouldn't necessarily paint what they see. Let's give you an example. I'm sitting on the river bank and on my left there's a specimen tree, and on the right bank there's a group of trees going into the distance, following the river as it bends to the left behind the tree. All the tones in the foliage appear to be the same. Now, I know from experience that if I paint what I see, the painting won't work. What I have to do is paint the tree on the left bank twice as dark as it appears.

The foreground tree on the right bank needs to be painted two-thirds as dark as the specimen tree. As the trees become more distant, you need to paint them gradually lighter in tone until the tree farthest in the distance passes behind the dark specimen tree on the left. This will achieve a sense of recession in the painting, leading your eye into the scene, along the river and out behind the specimen tree.

I used to spend hours visiting exhibitions, studying the work of other artists who painted similar scenes to mine. I asked myself why their paintings looked better. I soon realized that it was the distribution of light and dark values that made their paintings a success. If you follow this approach, I'll guarantee your paintings will improve significantly.

CHECK-LIST

• Water and reflections are constantly changing with the weather.

• A slight breeze will have a significant effect on the surface of water. Don't attempt to alter your painting as changes occur. Create a picture in your mind and paint from that.

• It's a good idea after painting the sky to carry the colours down into the water. When reflecting elements are involved in the landscape, paint the water in last, followed by their reflections.

• River banks are seldom straight like a road. Paint them to look 'ragged' for realism, adding shadows from the bank to give depth to the scene.

• Don't forget the principles of linear perspective. When painting the river banks, they should be wider in the foreground, gradually becoming narrower or vanishing in the distance.

• Paint the surrounding terrain first, allowing space for the water, then paint this in using the minimum of quick, light, positive strokes, leaving some paper uncovered to represent white water.

This painting of a Lakeland beck embraces some of the points in the check-list, and the techniques you'll practise in the exercises. I used fast, light strokes of the hake, which was loaded with varying tones of Payne's Gray/Cerulean Blue, to create the effect of fast-flowing water.

EXERCISES

1. Practise using a hake brush to paint tumbling water. Aim for quick strokes that lightly touch the paper. You will have to add darker tones but don't forget to leave lots of white paper showing through.

2. Practise the techniques for creating sparkle on the water (see pages 30–31).

3. Practise wet into wet reflections and, using a paper wedge, wipe out a wind line.

4. There's no substitute for painting outdoors. Sit by a river or waterfall, soak in the atmosphere, squint your eyes to identify the main patterns of flow and produce tonal studies from different vantage points.

How to transfer an outline drawing of a completed painting onto watercolour paper

The technique I'm about to tell you about is not a substitute for learning to draw and should only be used until you are competent at drawing.

1. Take a black and white photocopy of the painting to the size required.

2. Using a soft pencil (6B), scribble across the back of the photocopy.

3. Position the photocopy over your watercolour paper, trace around the outline and key features using a biro or 2H pencil.

4. Remove the photocopy. The image will have transferred to your paper ready for you to apply paint.

PAINTING WATER *Project*

Autumn Flow is the type of scene that makes being an artist so exciting. At the time, I was painting a lake scene and had noticed water running into the lake from an unknown source. Having completed my sketch, I decided to explore.

Imagine my surprise when I discovered this lovely woodland stream flowing between clusters of rock. I just had to sketch and photograph the scene to give me the basis for this stage-by-stage for you to paint.

1. THE ROCKS

The most difficult and time-consuming task was the positioning and painting of the rocks. I started by drawing the outlines using a brown water soluble crayon and painting in a loose wet into wet back-ground.

The rocks were painted with a ³/₄in flat brush. I used Raw Sienna washes to outline the rocks and while this was still wet added Burnt Sienna and finally darker tones of Payne's Gray/Alizarin Crimson.

When the paint was dry, I added some highlights to the rocks with a softened white water-soluble crayon. The fissures in the rocks were painted using a rigger brush.

2. THE TREES

The background trees were painted wet into wet and when the shine had gone from the paper I scratched in a few light tree structures with my thumb-nail. I could have used a palette knife but my thumb is always handy!

When the paint was dry, I put in the tree structures, using a rigger brush loaded with various mixes of Payne's Gray/Burnt Sienna. Then I stippled in the foliage using a sponge dipped in Burnt Sienna and Permanent Sap Green. The ivy was added to the trunks and more detail painted on the river banks.

3. THE WATER

Painting the water is the simplest and quickest part of this painting. I used light, quick, short strokes with the 1½ in hake brush loaded with mixes of Payne's Gray/Cerulean Blue; see page 30 for an explanation of this technique. I used the corner of the hake brush for the narrow flows and its full width for the wider flows. Initially I applied lighter tones and when these were dry followed with darker tones. The final stage was to add a little Raw Sienna to colour the water.

A WORD ABOUT DRAWING

When preparing an initial drawing it's important that you draw the scene correctly. In **Autumn Flow**, for example, the positioning of the rocks would be quite tricky for the less skilled.

Excessive erasing of pencil marks on the watercolour paper you are using for your painting can damage the surface. It is a good idea, therefore, to make your drawing on a separate piece of paper, correct it, and then – using the approach described on page 37 – transfer it to your watercolour paper. There's no need to take a photocopy in this instance.

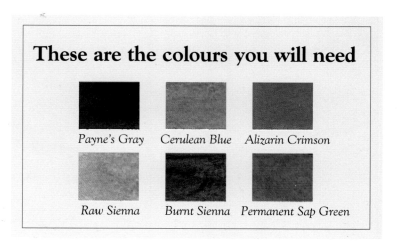

These are the colours you will need

Payne's Gray   Cerulean Blue   Alizarin Crimson

Raw Sienna   Burnt Sienna   Permanent Sap Green

PAINTING WATER *Project*

The landscape shown in **Tumbling Water** is typical of those found in the Yorkshire Dales National Park. It isn't my intention to show you how to paint the scene as a whole but rather to concentrate on how to create the effect of fast-flowing water as it tumbles over rocks. The land in this part of the country is quite peaty which colours the water a warm Sienna as it runs over the rocky shelves.

1. ESTABLISHING FLOW PATTERNS

As always, my approach was to complete a tonal study to determine the most appropriate vantage point. This study helped me to clarify my approach to the painting, to identify the most important flow patterns and to establish the light and dark values. The water is so complex, you need to simplify.

Using the hake brush, I initially made a few marks to identify the principal flow patterns. I used a rigger brush to paint in a few small rocks using a weak Payne's Gray wash.

2. BUILDING UP THE WATER

Using horizontal strokes with the side of the size 14 round brush and a weak Cerulean Blue mix, I painted in the water, being careful to leave some of the white paper uncovered.

The next step was to give more definition to the water flowing between the rocks, using the corner of the hake brush loaded with a Payne's Gray/Cerulean Blue mix. To create this effect you need just 'twitch' the brush; in other words, depositing the paint by using fast short strokes. (It's a good idea to practise on a similar type of watercolour paper first until you are happy that the paint is being deposited as you wish.) A weak Burnt Sienna was brushed in to represent the colour of peaty water.

3. ADDING DEPTH AND DETAIL

All that's left to do is to paint in some darker tones of Payne's Gray to add depth and detail to the water flowing away from the base of the rocks.

It's inevitable, when painting water, that you will get carried away and overdo it in places. In my case, I hadn't left sufficient white paper showing through between the rock on the right and the bank. This can easily be corrected by dipping a hog-hair brush into clean water and washing off the paint, then dabbing the area with a tissue to restore the white paper. Simpler still is to try the technique I have used here: take a white water-soluble crayon and add a few white streaks.

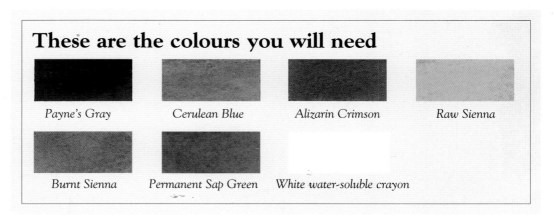

Adding interest

You will notice that I have positioned a few sheep in this painting. They make such a difference to the foreground and add life to the painting.

These are the colours you will need

Payne's Gray	Cerulean Blue	Alizarin Crimson	Raw Sienna
Burnt Sienna	Permanent Sap Green	White water-soluble crayon	

85

TREES, ROCKS and RUNNING WATER *Linear perspective*

In this painting I want you to take note of how I have ensured linear perspective. First the brush strokes are directed towards the vanishing point; secondly, the river bank is shaped so that it is wider in the foreground and narrow in the distance; and finally the trees gradually diminish in height as they recede into the distance. By these principles of linear perspective the eye is led into the painting, through to its furthest point where the river vanishes out of sight round the bend.

SHAPING THE RIVER BANK

If you make your river banks a feature of your painting it will look more interesting. Don't paint them as straight lines. The bank will have land jutting out into the water and inlets where the water, with time, has washed away the soil. In this example you'll see that I've painted in some dark shadows or reflections to give the water depth and interest. Adding a few rocks also helps to create a pleasing effect.

THE ROCKS

The shadows on and under the rocks were achieved by applying darker tones of a Payne's Gray/Alizarin Crimson mix with a ³/₄ in one stroke brush. When the paint was one-third dry, I moved it around with a palette knife to give the rocks a realistic look. When the painting was completely dry, I used a softened white water-soluble crayon to add the effect of a little snow.

THE WATER

The reflections from the trees were painted wet into wet, using downward strokes with a flat brush loaded with the tree colours (Raw Sienna, Burnt Sienna, Payne's Gray, Alizarin Crimson, Permanent Sap Green and Burnt Umber). The wind lines were made by removing some of the paint by means of a tissue shaped to a wedge. Burnt Umber applied with a rigger brush was used to paint the reflections of some of the trees.

THE TREES AND BANK

The trees lining the bank vary in shape, height and variety. Two firs stand out, however. They were painted with the rocking, stippling technique described on page 15. The remaining trees/bushes were painted using a size 16 hog-hair brush with a stippling action. The snow on the trees was added by stippling with white acrylic paint. The distant trees have been loosely painted in very pale, cool colours to achieve recession in the painting.

Some of the sky colours (Payne's Gray, Alizarin Crimson, Cerulean Blue) were introduced into the bank by wetting the white of the paper with clean water and letting the subtle touches of colour blend in.

TREES, ROCKS and RUNNING WATER *Experimenting with media*

This atmospheric landscape, which I call **Seldom Seen**, provides an opportunity to show a range of more unusual techniques. The more successful artist will be continually experimenting with new techniques to improve their work. I hope you find this method of working stretches your imagination.

MASKING AND POURING PAINT

After drawing a simple outline I applied masking fluid by means of a piece of crumpled grease-proof paper and lightly dabbed it on the areas of foliage that I wanted to preserve. By shaping a piece of grease-proof paper to a point, I masked the river bank and areas of the water. For fine lines in the water and the tree structures, I used a cocktail stick dipped in masking. These aids were disposable, saving me the task of cleaning brushes.

Generous washes of Raw Sienna, Permanent Sap Green, Cadmium Yellow Pale, Payne's Gray and a Payne's Gray/Alizarin Crimson mix were mixed in saucers in readiness for pouring when the masking had dried.

The paper was inclined at an angle of 10 degrees, Cadmium Yellow Pale poured on the right-hand side and Permanent Sap Green on the left-hand side. The paper was then tilted until it was almost vertical, allowing the colours to blend and run off the bottom of the paper.

While the paint was still wet, I used a tissue shaped to a wedge and stroked upwards from the base of the fall, removing paint, to represent water spray.

The wind lines were created by wiping a wedge-shaped tissue across the water. The paint was then allowed to dry.

ADDING DARKER TONES

A further pouring of Payne's Gray/Alizarin Crimson was completed to darken the area around the waterfall. The wash was allowed to run off the bottom of the painting to darken the water.

When the wash was dry, I used a putty eraser to remove the masking fluid.

CREATING TEXTURE

A Cadmium Yellow Pale wash was poured down the right-hand side to brighten the foliage and a sap green wash down the left to darken the foliage. The paint was allowed to dry. This was followed by re-wetting selected areas of the right-hand foliage with clean water, using a spray bottle. Texture was created by 'spattering' with Cadmium Yellow Pale. I tapped a well laden brush across the handle to achieve this effect; how hard you tap and how far away you are from the paper determines the size of the droplets. Where the paint hits dry paper, distinct highlights will result and

where it hits dampened paper the effect will be blurred images and a softer texture.

I applied a Raw Sienna wash to the river bank and the whole of the water area. Texture to represent rough grass was painted on the bank and a purple wash applied to selected areas of the water to darken the tonal value, creating a pleasing shadow.

FINAL TOUCHES

To complete the painting, further detail was added to the foliage by applying a lighter Cadmium Yellow Pale/Raw Sienna mix. A Payne's Gray/Alizarin Crimson glaze was applied to the left-hand area of water and to the rocks. Finally, I felt that the addition of the fence would improve the composition.

These are the colours you will need

Payne's Gray *Alizarin Crimson* *Raw Sienna* *Cadmium Yellow Pale* *Permanent Sap Green*

TREES, ROCKS and RUNNING WATER *Close up*

I chose **Sunburst** for you to study because it shows background light shining through the trees and reflecting on the surface of the water.

THE BACKGROUND

The background has been painted wet into wet to create recession in the painting. Snow is very rarely pure white. It reflects cloud shadows and effects of the light. Raw or Burnt Sienna can be used to give the snow a warmer look, as in this painting. For a 'cold' snow scene I use pale blue shadows.

To paint the sky area, I applied various tones of Cerulean Blue and immediately painted in Payne's Gray/Alizarin Crimson, Cadmium Yellow Pale and Burnt Sienna washes to selected areas. I added darker tones of Payne's Gray/Permanent Sap Green to represent the bushes in the background. To achieve this soft, atmospheric effect, I had to work quickly, while the sky was still quite wet.

Once the shine had gone from the paper, the tree structures were scratched out with a palette knife. Timing is important here. If you scratch out when the paint is very wet the area will fill in and turn a darker tone but if you time it just right, you will reveal the white paper. Here, I have achieved a mixture of both – light areas of trunk with darker edging that gives the trees authenticity.

THE BANK AND REFLECTIONS

Notice the pleasing shape of the bank and how subtle colours and tufts of grass have been added for interest. After shaping the bank, I added darker reflections in the water. For these I used a mix of Payne's Gray/Permanent Sap Green and at the edges added a little Burnt Sienna.

I used the tissue wedge technique to indicate wind lines in the water.

The snow on the trees – and particularly the bush – was stippled in, using a hog-hair brush dipped in white acrylic paint. I scratched in the tree structures with my thumb-nail.

THE FIR TREES

I painted an initial weak Permanent Sap Green wash as background. The fir trees were painted with a flat brush using a rocking action (see page 15). For the trees, I used strong mixes of Payne's Gray/Permanent Sap Green and added a little Burnt Sienna in selected areas to provide variation.

It was important to paint darker tones for the tree group on the left-hand bank to take the eye along the river and round the bend. The painting would have looked flat if I had painted this group in lighter tones.

ATMOSPHERE, MOOD & LIGHT

LIGHT *Introduction*

Artists of all generations have endeavoured to capture the magical effects of light on the landscape. Watercolour painting is ideal for this by providing contrasting tonal values and colour, wet into wet and the ability to incorporate both hard and soft edges.

Coloured glazes consisting of a small amount of paint and lots of water can easily be applied, either to warm up sections of a painting to represent sunlight or to provide contrast by applying cool colours.

It's important to realize that the white of the paper and the transparency of watercolour provide the greatest source of light in a watercolour painting. A source of light can be brightened by surrounding it with darker contrasting tones of colour. You can prove this for yourself: take a piece of waste watercolour paper, paint your light source, then paint dark tones of colour around it. If you do this your light source will appear lighter.

To begin with it's a good idea to select your subject and produce simple tonal studies to visualize the effects of light on your landscape. If you paint your subject at different times of the day, you will experience the effect changing light has on the landscape. The knowledge you get from these exercises will be invaluable for your paintings.

The colours I find most useful are shown below.

Payne's Gray

Cadmium Yellow Pale

Cerulean Blue

Alizarin Crimson

Raw Sienna

Burnt Umber

In **Evening Light** *I used various tonal values in the clouds on the right and left lighter areas surrounding the large tree, to emphasize its structure. I painted cloud shadows in the foreground to provide contrast with the soft light in the sky.*

Moonlight *provides a good example of light in the landscape. The soft light radiates over the distant mountains and highlights the farmstead and the track, leading the viewer's eye into the painting. Masking fluid was initially applied to preserve the white of the paper representing the track. Washes and detail were applied after the masking fluid was removed.*

Practice
- *Study the examples in this book and practise painting wet into wet skies to represent the various light situations.*
- *Practise colour mixing, using the colours specified in the text.*
- *Practise using an eraser to remove colour, creating shafts of light as in a woodland glade or an atmospheric sky.*

Colour has fascinated artists for generations. Many books have been written about this subject but there's no substitute for experience. I'm often asked by my students to divulge the percentages of each hue I have mixed together to achieve a particular colour, but I can't tell them. I just mix quantities of each colour together until I am satisfied with the outcome. Certain rules obviously have to be followed. If fresh clean colours are required, it's best to mix only two colours together. For more subtle shades, mix three colours together. If you mix more than three colours you are likely to end up with a dull colour. Artists call this 'mud', but there may be occasions when this is precisely what is needed.

THE BASICS OF COLOUR MIXING

The primary colours are red, yellow and blue. If similar quantities of each primary colour are mixed together the result is almost a black colour, as shown in the colour circle left. If blue and yellow are mixed together, they will produce green. Mixing red and yellow gives orange, while mixing red and blue results in a violet or purple colour. These mixtures are known as secondary colours. Tertiary colours are created by mixing a primary colour with a secondary colour; any red, yellow and blue will suffice. It's easy, as the next exercise shows.

Follow the arrows in the colour circle. By using three primary colours in the above combinations with various amounts of water, a wide range of tints can be produced. Of course, a vast range of colours can be bought, but there's nothing like experimenting with the basics to discover the range of tones you can produce.

Some colour combinations I find useful are shown below.

Cerulean Blue and Alizarin Crimson –
Shadows over snow

Raw Sienna and Alizarin Crimson –
Under-painting for evening sky

Payne's Gray and Alizarin Crimson –
Cloud colours for evening sky

Payne's Gray and Cerulean Blue –
Rain clouds

Payne's Gray and Raw Sienna –
Mist and fog

My basic palette of colours is shown below. The beginner won't go far wrong if they begin with this selection. Additional colours I use to support my basic palette are also shown below. I call these extra colours my 'supportive' palette. Occasionally, I may select further colours from the wide range available.

Basic palette: Payne's Gray, Cerulean Blue, Alizarin Crimson, Raw Sienna, Burnt Sienna, Burnt Umber, Cadmium Yellow Pale, Permanent Sap Green.

Supportive palette: French Ultramarine, Indanthrene Blue, Quinacridone Red, Winsor Yellow, Brown Madder Alizarin, Gold Ochre.

Payne's Gray and Alizarin Crimson – storm clouds

Alizarin Crimson and Cerulean Blue – cloud colours

Payne's Gray and Burnt Umber – storm clouds

French Ultramarine and Cadmium Yellow Pale – light in the sky

Storm clouds – Payne's Gray and Alizarin Crimson, painted over a pale Raw Sienna wash.

Light on the landscape – French Ultramarine on the right and French Ultramarine/Alizarin Crimson on the left, painted over a Cadmium Yellow Pale under-painting.

LIGHT Colour Mixing *Practice*

I've included this woodland scene, **Coat of Many Colours**, to provide you with an opportunity to practise your colour mixing. I would like you to note the variations in tone throughout this painting – this variation is important. The tree grouping on the left side of the painting has been painted in darker tones, leading the eye beyond it and into the distance.

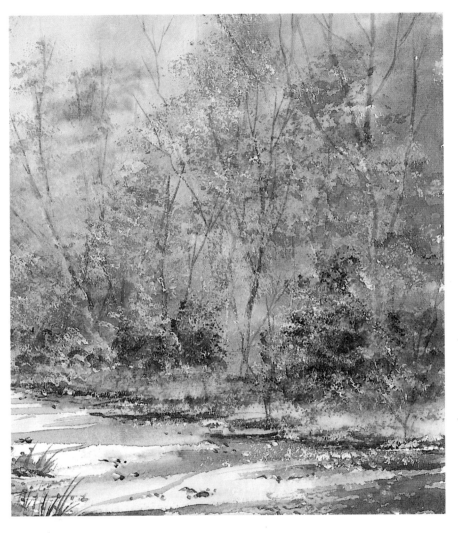

AUTUMN TREES

In this grouping you will observe a wide range of green and autumn tints. The greens have been created by using Cerulean Blue mixed with Cadmium Yellow Pale and Raw Sienna. The autumn hues have been mixed using combinations of Raw Sienna, Burnt Sienna and Alizarin Crimson.

Trees and bushes appear dark on the inside and become lighter towards the extremities. To capture this depth in the foliage, I over-painted with dark tones of Payne's Gray mixed with a little Alizarin Crimson when the under-painting was completely dry, producing a dark mauve colour. Never use black for this purpose – it really kills a painting.

The tree structures were painted using a weak Burnt Umber, followed by stippling in the foliage with a small, artist's sponge, incorporating suitable autumn colours. Before you try this, practise first on a similarly textured piece of watercolour paper.

ADDING DARKER TONES

To create the foliage on the left-hand trees, I applied a wide range of greens in varying tones, mixed from Cerulean Blue, Cadmium Yellow and Raw Sienna. To paint the foliage, I stippled with the sponge dipped in paint, pre-mixed on my palette. When this was completely dry, I over-stippled with dark tones of a Payne's Gray/Alizarin Crimson mix to create depth in the foliage. Depth is so necessary to the success of a painting such as this, because it leads the eye beyond the darker tree grouping into the distance. This concept or design principle is known as 'recession'.

When the paint was dry I added some white gouache paint to the green mixtures to lighten them. Using the stippling technique, I added a few highlights in the foliage to retain the overall impression of depth.

TEXTURE

Your painting can be made more realistic by adding texture to the grassy areas. This is achieved by applying initial washes of a soft pale yellow in the distance, followed by green to selected areas. When the paint is approximately half dry, the edge of a hake (the tip of the brush should be brought almost to a chisel edge) is used to paint in some darker tones to represent texture; loading the brush with a Payne's Gray/Alizarin Crimson mix is ideal for this. You must touch the paper lightly to deposit paint, then, using the corner of the brush, flick upwards to create tufts of grass. It's a very simple technique.

The walkers are important in this painting – they're the focal point, leading your eye down the path. Don't forget to paint some shadows across the footpath.

LIGHT *Design considerations*

When I first began painting, I often completed paintings that looked boring although drawn correctly and well designed. After studying works of art in national galleries, I soon realized that my paintings needed light to give them life. Light is the single most important factor in all paintings.

When I'm unhappy with a painting, I will shine a powerful torch over it to determine whether making areas lighter will improve my representation. Then I wash out the colour with a sponge and dab it with a tissue until I feel I've created the effect I'm looking for. Try this technique – it works.

Although I still use this technique, I attempt to plan for it before I apply paint. Paintings don't just happen, they have to be designed. Keep the following points in mind when you are planning your painting.

Points to Remember

1. *In early morning light, shadows are ill-defined, the elements lack sharpness and colours have a bluish appearance.*

2. *When the sun is setting every feature in the landscape – eg, buildings, trees, etc – will appear as silhouettes against the sky.*

3. *Glazes can be applied to warm certain areas of a painting to represent sunlight.*

Winter's Majesty *is a very simple exercise for you to try. Note the cold winter sky, the splashes of colour in the foliage and the sense of recession, achieved by painting the far distant trees in pale cool colours wet into wet. Observe the subtle sky shadows in the snow and the impression of stubble here and there. The figures are the focal point. The tree structures were scratched out with a palette knife and cocktail stick when the paint was one-third dry.*

There's something special about light attempting to show through the diffused background of early morning mist. The atmospheric effect makes it difficult to see the real colours of objects in the distance.

In the middle distance, colours appear bluer, less sharply defined and lighter in tone, no matter how much light there is. As we approach the foreground the elements appear sharper and darker in tone than they do in the distance. Although their true colours are displayed, foreground objects can appear simply as silhouettes if the distant light is bright.

In **The Hikers** *the principles of design we addressed above are clearly represented. The light is attempting to break through the mist and the distant mountains are diffused and cool in colour. The path leads the eye into the painting and the hikers become the focal point. More detail has been painted in the foreground, with the rocks created by outlining their shape with brushwork and their structure scratched out with a palette knife.*

Autumn on the Lake *was a simple sketch produced in six minutes. The group of trees is virtually a silhouette, but colour reflects across the loch as the sun rises above the distant mountains. This is a useful exercise for a beginner.*

Here are three different examples of early morning light: first light as dawn breaks; a back-lit subject where the light has broken through the clouds, creating a glow over distant mountains; and a front-lit woodland scene.

Skylight *is a fine example of early morning sun breaking through the clouds, lighting up the landscape. The distant mountain seems to sparkle, as does the surface of the water. The sky is the main feature in this painting, although it was painted in less than three minutes. Initially, I painted a circle of Cadmium Yellow Pale. While the paper was flat, I painted French Ultramarine on the right-hand side and a Payne's Gray/Alizarin Crimson mix on the left.*

Using a spray bottle, I sprayed water in the centre of the Cadmium Yellow Pale and, lifting up the board, tilted the paper to allow the colours to run in different directions and blend together. An occasional spray here and there encouraged the paint to flow freely. When I was satisfied with the cloud formation, I laid the board perfectly flat to allow the paint to dry. When approximately one-third dry, I used an absorbent tissue to add a few white clouds.

Boathouse *was painted at the first light of dawn. The background is a simple wash of varying light tones of Payne's Gray over a weak Raw Sienna under-painting. The distant trees were painted wet into wet to achieve a soft diffused look. The foreground trees are in silhouette. The red roof of the boathouse is quite dull, as is the pale coloured stonework. The lake surface reflects the colours of the sky and the water on the left-hand side is in shadow from the dark tree grouping. The boat was added to give a splash of colour to this otherwise dull scene.*

River Rhapsody *is the type of scene I love to paint. The subdued early morning light was behind me, attempting to break through the early morning mist. The far distant trees can barely be seen and blurred images of the trees in the middle distance provide a background to the large trees on the left.*

It's autumn, the leaves have fallen, allowing the structure of the trees to be visible. Distant tree structures were scratched out with the palette knife. If the paint is too wet when scratched out it will run back, resulting in a dark tree structure. The trick is to leave the paint until it is about one-third dry, when a pleasing light tree structure will result. In this painting some structures are light and others dark.

The trunks of the large trees in the foreground were painted

in dark tones of brown and a tissue shaped to a point wiped down to remove paint, lightening the right-hand side of the trunks. A rigger brush was used to paint some dark tones on the trunks, making them look round. The branches were added – also using a rigger brush – and a few reflections painted in the water.

Very important in this painting are the contrasts of pale tones and colours representing the soft, diffused early morning atmosphere.

LIGHT *Evening*

Evening is probably my favourite time to paint. The landscape is going to sleep. It's so peaceful, a time for contemplation. The clouds have darkened, contrasting with the light in the sky, making the light appear even brighter. The sky colours are reflected on the surface of the water, creating a sense of peace and tranquillity.

In **Lone Sailor** the silhouettes of the foreground rocks and the sailor contrast with the fading light.

I want you to use your imagination to try to capture this scene in paint. Don't try to copy the colours I have used exactly. Use them only as guides. Make the painting your own. Have some fun with it.

Soft Light *contrasts with the painting above, the light soft and diffused, providing a glowing background to this autumn scene. I painted the sky by initially applying a pale Raw Sienna wash to wet the whole of the painting. In the sky, I brushed in soft purple mixes made from Payne's Gray and Alizarin Crimson, adding lots of water to produce the pastel colours. While the paint was still wet, I brushed in some pale grey to represent distant trees.*

The ivy covering the base of the trees was painted by stippling various green tones with a round headed hog-hair brush. This brush was also used to stipple in the foreground texture after the initial wash had dried. (For detailed instructions on painting tree structures, see page 43.)

The sea is calm, the day's fishing is over and the light is quickly fading. The scene depicted in **Resting** was completed in 40 minutes on the coastal road near Mallaig in Scotland.

An initial Raw Sienna wash was applied to the sky area with a hake brush. I added a little Alizarin Crimson as I worked towards the horizon. When the under-painting was approximately one-third dry, the clouds were painted using mixes of Payne's Gray and Alizarin Crimson. The same colours were used to paint the water.

The boat was added to balance the darker cloud formations in the left-hand side of the painting, but it's the sky that establishes the atmosphere and mood.

The treetops and a distant field are illuminated in **Moonlight**. I began by painting the full moon with masking fluid. When this was completely dry, I painted the sky by wetting the paper with clean water, using the hake brush, and followed this with washes of French Ultramarine with a little Alizarin Crimson added. A tissue was used to create a few white cloud shapes. When the rest of the painting was completed, the masking was removed and the shadows on the moon were painted. Note that the path was painted by retaining the white of the paper and adding a little colour here and there. It's an important feature, leading the eye into the painting and up to the moon.

Walk on the Beach shows a glorious sky lighting up the landscape. I used a range of colours to capture it. In addition to soft Cerulean Blue and Raw Sienna, with a touch of Gold Ochre for the under-painting, I used a combination of Payne's Gray/Cerulean Blue and Burnt Sienna for the clouds. A tissue was used to soften the edges and create a few white clouds. The sea was painted with a hake brush. I painted the rocks initially by applying washes and then created the shapes by moving paint with a palette knife. Note the shadows over the sand – such little touches improve a painting.

LIGHT *Project*

The scene depicted in **The Garden in Bloom** is one that I felt I just had to paint, as a reminder of my visit to Bodnant Gardens in Wales. The soft blue sky contrasted beautifully with the colourful azaleas and rhododendrons. I remember sitting on a seat, thinking how peaceful it was. The painting provided the opportunity to use some imaginative techniques to achieve the end result.

1. DRAWING AND MASKING

I drew a rough outline with a dark brown water-soluble crayon and, using masking fluid, masked the tree structures using a twig for the trunks and a cocktail stick for the finer lines. These tools were disposable, which saved me the effort of having to remove the masking from brushes. I used a stippling action with a crumpled piece of grease-proof paper dipped in the fluid to mask the foliage. To paint the sky, I poured a Cerulean Blue wash over the area, followed by a Permanent Sap Green wash over the areas of foliage. Both of these washes were pre-mixed in ceramic saucers.

2. BUILDING UP TONE

In order to represent shadows in the foliage, I waited until the washes in stage 1 had completely dried and then poured a dark tone of pre-mixed Permanent Sap Green/Burnt Umber over the lower half of the painting.

3. REMOVING MASKING AND PAINTING THE BUSHES

After removing the masking from the trees and bushes above the bridge by means of a putty eraser, I painted in representations of azaleas and rhododendrons. The colours I used were mixes of Raw Sienna, Cadmium Yellow Pale, Alizarin Crimson and Burnt Sienna, applied with a size 6 round brush.

4. REMOVING MASKING, PAINTING FLOWERS AND WATER

The masking was removed from the lower half of the painting and the flowers painted with mixes of French Ultramarine, Alizarin Crimson, Raw Sienna, Cadmium Yellow Pale, Burnt Sienna and Payne's Gray. Payne's Gray and Alizarin Crimson provided a darker tone as shadows in the foreground bushes. The stream was painted using various tones of a Cerulean Blue/Payne's Gray mix.

5. FINAL STAGE

To complete this painting the background trees were added, using darker tones of green for the left-hand tree and lighter tones for the right-hand tree. A range of soft yellow greens and darker greens were mixed using Cadmium Yellow Pale and Permanent Sap Green. A natural sponge dipped in the mixes was used to stipple in the foliage. A rigger brush loaded with Burnt Umber was used to paint in the tree structures.

The colours used

| Payne's Gray | Cerulean Blue | Alizarin Crimson | Raw Sienna | Burnt Umber | Cadmium Yellow Pale | Permanent Sap Green | Burnt Sienna |

ATMOSPHERE AND MOOD *Introduction*

There's an old saying that 'labourers work with their hands, craftsmen work with their hands and their head, and artists work with their hands, head and *heart*.' This is particularly relevant when creating atmosphere and mood.

Emotions can be stirred by a fast-flowing river, the beauty of falling snow, the effect of light, children playing on a beach or the excitement of colour in a landscape.

Creating atmosphere and mood isn't just attempting to capture a sense of drama such as wind-blown clouds over a dominant mountain structure. It may be a sense of peace and tranquillity, a pastoral scene or the shape of trees in a particular setting. It's what stirs our emotions and provides us with a sense of excitement, contentment, fascination or awe.

It's the artist's role to attempt to capture that special moment in time, using the tools at his disposal.

Diagonal lines provide a sense of movement, as in a wind-blown sky. Vertical lines suggest a sense of awe and power, such as in tall buildings or high mountains. Horizontal lines suggest a pastoral scene. An atmospheric effect can be subtle or bold but the overall effect should be representative of the place you are painting and sympathetic to nature.

In the following pages, I'm going to show you how to paint a wide range of atmospheric effects and encourage you to use your imagination to create paintings that will give you many years of pleasure and satisfaction.

Painting is rather like making a cake – gather all the ingredients together in the best mix and create your masterpiece.

I painted this evening sky, **From the Road to Mallaig,** *by initially applying a Cerulean Blue wash at the top and adding a Raw Sienna/Alizarin Crimson mix as I approached the horizon. When the under-painting was approximately one-third dry, the clouds were painted, using the hake brush loaded with a dark toned Payne's Gray/Alizarin Crimson mix.*

Points to remember

- *Try to create a wide range of atmospheric effects.*
- *Use your imagination.*

The tonal values on the left side of this typical woodland path in **Green Harmony** are darker than those on the right. In the distance the colours are paler and cooler, taking the viewer's eye down the path into the painting. The walkers are the focal point and have been placed to direct the eye.

The colours used

Payne's Gray   Cerulean Blue   Alizarin Crimson   Raw Sienna   Burnt Umber   Cadmium Yellow Pale   Permanent Sap Green   Burnt Sienna

ATMOSPHERE AND MOOD *The effect of light*

It can be an informative and enjoyable experience to paint the same scene at different times of the day. The changing light has significant effects on the landscape, creating contrasts in atmosphere and mood. Compare these paintings of the same scene in early morning, at midday and in early evening.

Early Morning *Blue-green mixes and simple washes were used here to clearly define the time of day.*

The shadows are ill-defined, and the subtle distinctions between the elements lack sharpness. The colours tend to a bluish green and there's a suggestion of mist that will quickly disappear as the sun rises.

I painted a wet into wet sky, using Cerulean Blue, and added a weak Permanent Sap Green to the blue to paint the distant trees. Various tones of these two colours were used to paint the foreground trees and bushes, the land and also the water.

Midday *The clarity of this landscape suggests that it's noon. Any early morning mist has been burnt off by the warmth of the sun. A division between the lights and darks can easily be seen. There's a greater contrast in colours and tones because the light is stronger.*

I used combinations of French Ultramarine, Cadmium Yellow Pale, Raw Sienna and a Payne's Gray for the trees and painted warmer colours in the land areas. The sunlight is reflected in the water.

Late Evening *The sun is beginning to set. The elements are silhouetted against the warmth of the sky and there's less detail to be seen. The water reflects the colours of the sky. Night is rapidly approaching. In a short time the landscape will fade into darkness. Everything is at rest; the birds have gone to roost and the fishermen are enjoying peace and quiet, away from the stresses of life.*

The colours I used to paint this scene were Cadmium Yellow Pale, Raw Sienna, Alizarin Crimson and Burnt Umber.

EXERCISES

• Select a local scene, within your present competence level, and paint it at different times of the day. Make notes of the principal differences in terms of light, cloud structures, colour contrasts, tonal values and sharpness.

• Take lots of photographs of interesting cloud formations to build up a resource from which you can draw as and when required.

• Study the effect rain clouds have on the colours in the landscape.

• Choose a landscape painting in this book and paint it as if it were a depiction of another season.

• Practise painting sheep, figures and boats.

Autumn Light *depicts the changing colours of autumn. Note the variety of colours in the foliage and the effect of light in the atmospheric sky radiating over the mountain range.*

Because this is a back-lit subject, shadows are cast in the water.

Points to remember

• An atmospheric effect can be subtle or bold, but the overall impression should be representative of the region and sympathetic to nature.
• When painting early morning, shadows are ill-defined and the subtle distinctions between the elements lack sharpness.
• In the evening shapes become silhouettes against a soft, warm sky.
• The sky sets the scene in a painting, creating atmosphere and mood.

• Fog and mist cast a veil over distant objects; colours are softened and the elements appear diffused. Distant fog or mist can be emphasized by adding in the foreground a little more detail and colour than can actually be seen.
• When painting snow always establish the value relationships between the sky and its reflections in the snow.
• To paint rain, apply a wet initial wash, paint in the cloud colours, lift the board and tilt it to encourage the paint to run in the direction required. When you are satisfied with the result, lay the board flat and allow the paint to dry naturally.

ATMOSPHERE AND MOOD *Skies and rain clouds*

The sky establishes the atmosphere and mood in a painting. The effects of light in the landscape are vital to bring your watercolours to life. Don't forget that practice makes perfect – you're not expected to get it right first time.

When I want to emphasize the effects of light in the landscape and to help me create atmosphere and mood, I will take photographs that go against the usual conventions of photography. Rather than having the sun behind me as convention dictates, I will shoot looking directly into the sun. The photographs will print much darker but the contrasting lights and darks will be very distinctive. I will use different camera settings, and then assess the results.

Try this approach for yourself. When you come to apply paint to your subject, it will be up to you to create the atmosphere and mood you want.

The sky in **Scottish Loch** *was painted with the same technique as that used in* **Snow Capped**. *The colours used were Raw Sienna, French Ultramarine and Alizarin Crimson.*

Snow Capped *is a dramatic sky painted with a hake brush. A circle of Cadmium Yellow Pale was painted to represent light radiating from the sun. Mixes of Cerulean Blue/Payne's Gray and Alizarin Crimson were used to paint various tones of colour in the sky. While the paint was still very wet the paper was tilted to allow the colours to flow and blend together.*

The dramatic sky in **Not Quite There** *was painted in less than four minutes. A greater variety of colours and tones was used for this sky study than for the other two shown on this page: Raw Sienna for the under-painting, followed by Cerulean/French Ultramarine mixes and Payne's Gray/Alizarin Crimson to create the darker tones. A few white clouds were created by removing paint with an absorbent tissue.*

A sky full of rain is possibly the easiest type to paint with watercolours. Attach your watercolour paper to a board and lay it flat, apply a very wet wash of a pale tone of Cerulean Blue or Raw Sienna and, while the paper is still very wet, brush in dark tones of Payne's Gray mixed with Raw Sienna, Burnt Umber or Alizarin Crimson at the top of your paper. Immediately, lift up the board and paper and, holding them almost vertical, tilt them in the direction required to encourage the paint to flow. Watch the result as you do this, and once the paint has run sufficiently to create the effect you're looking for, lay the paper perfectly flat and let the paint dry naturally. Use a tissue to soak up any unwanted pools of colour at the bottom of the sky. It's as easy as that.

This technique was used for both of the paintings shown below.

Homeward Bound *was started in the English Lake District while my wife held an umbrella over me. Such weather conditions encourage speedy work.*

For the sky, I quickly brushed in a weak Cerulean Blue and added a little Raw Sienna in selected areas, followed by a Payne's Gray/Raw Sienna mix. The shepherd and sheep were painted in my studio later.

The House on the Moor *offers you an opportunity to practise the technique I use for depicting a rainy landscape. Although the technique is very easy, timing is important. Only experience through practice will teach you how to get this right.*

To paint the sky, wet the area initially with a weak Raw Sienna or Cerulean Blue, and use a mix of Payne's Gray/Raw Sienna for the clouds.

ATMOSPHERE AND MOOD *Close up*

Wet and Windy is full of atmosphere and mood. The rain is streaking down. The distant mountains are barely discernible through the torrential rain and this gives them a ghostly appearance. It's not the day to be out and about. The smoke from the chimney indicates that those living in the croft are of the same opinion. I think you will enjoy painting this scene.

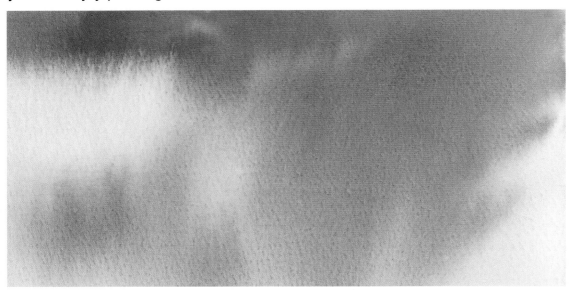

THE SKY

I fastened the paper to the board and laid it flat before painting the rain clouds. I used a hake brush to apply a very wet Cerulean Blue wash to the whole of the sky area. While the under-painting was still wet, a strong mix of Payne's Gray with a little Burnt Umber added was brushed into the top of the sky. The board was immediately lifted and angled vertically to allow the paint to run down the paper. Once the desired effect was achieved the board was laid perfectly flat and the paint left to dry naturally.

MOUNTAINS AND BUILDINGS

I fastened the paper to the board and laid it flat before painting the rain clouds. I used a hake brush to apply a very wet Cerulean Blue wash to the whole of the sky area. While the under-painting was still wet, a strong mix of Payne's Gray with a little Burnt Umber added was brushed into the top of the sky. The board was immediately lifted and angled vertically to allow the paint to run down the paper. Once the desired effect was achieved the board was laid perfectly flat and the paint left to dry naturally.

Atmosphere

In this painting the atmosphere is created almost entirely by the rain clouds and their effect on the landscape.

114

ROCKS

After removing the masking the rocks were painted using Raw Sienna as an under-painting and Payne's Gray/Burnt Umber for the shadows. Highlights were made by removing paint from the tops of the rocks with a tissue rolled to a point. Dark shadows were painted under the rocks to make them look more realistic.

ATMOSPHERE AND MOOD *Mist, fog and snow*

Fog and mist cast a veil over objects in the distance and colours appear soft and diffused. It's important to keep distant values light in tone and add a little more colour and definition in the foreground. The foreground must be more sharply focussed than it appears in reality to give emphasis to the mist or fog in the background

The sky for **Lakeside** *was painted wet into wet, by applying a weak Cerulean Blue wash and brushing in some Alizarin Crimson. I continued working downwards and painted the water using the same colours. While the paint was still wet, I painted the distant mountains and the trees in the middle distance, wet into wet, to achieve a soft diffused look. The fir trees were painted with a stiffer Permanent Sap Green, then I used a tissue to remove some colour and soften the tree grouping. Reflections using very pale colours were added to the water while the paint was still wet. When the paint was dry the land and rocks in the foreground were painted .in more detail to lead the viewer's eye into the painting.*

Mist on the River *depicts an early morning scene, with the sun struggling to shine through the mist. The sketch has been painted wet into wet to achieve the soft, filtered light effect that is so necessary when painting mist or fog. My aim was to create a hazy atmospheric effect. The colours used were Cadmium Yellow Pale, Raw Sienna, Payne's Gray, Alizarin Crimson, Cerulean Blue and Burnt Sienna.*

When painting snow it's important to establish the value relationships between the snow and the sky. Snow isn't always white, just as the sky is not always a pretty blue. Leave the paper untouched for the whitest snow. The washes used for the sky can be transferred to the snow area to create the shadows reflected from passing clouds.

Snow scenes don't have to look cold. You can use soft washes of Cerulean Blue for a cold scene, a purple hue made from Payne's Gray or French Ultramarine and Alizarin Crimson for a slightly warmer effect, and for warmer sunlit snow you can apply a Raw Sienna glaze over a blue or purple underpainting. Show some stubble, tufts of grass or even the odd rock protruding through the snow to add interest.

In the following two examples, you'll notice how important are the skies to the success of the paintings.

Early Snow *depicts the first coating of snow on the landscape. The subject is backlit; I have painted a little Raw Sienna into the sky to reflect this, and have also transferred some of this colour into the snow lying on the fields. Note how I have achieved recession by painting the trees and bushes in the far distance in cooler pale tones.*

To paint the stubble and vegetation showing through the light covering of snow, I used the edge of a hake brush, touching the paper lightly with an upward flicking motion.

In **On Thurstaston Hill**, *a favourite beauty spot in the Wirral, where I live, I have used the sky colours of Payne's Gray and Alizarin Crimson to paint the path and the pool of water on the right. This was important to achieve colour harmony in the scene. The white of the paper has been left uncovered to represent snow at ground level. I used a little white acrylic paint to stipple the effects of snow on the trees and foreground gorse bushes.*

ATMOSPHERE AND MOOD *Close up*

There's nothing quite like a walk in the woods on a crisp winter's day. Nature in all its glory is a joy to behold. **Woodland Walk** is one such scene, providing the opportunity to incorporate a soft atmospheric sky, a wide variation in the colours of winter and the effects of a light dusting of snow on the landscape. This is the type of scene I love to paint. I used acrylic watercolours to paint it.

SKY AND IVY

I painted the sky by initially applying a pale Raw Sienna wash over the sky area with a hake brush. Using downward strokes, I then brushed in Cerulean Blue, starting on the left and gradually changing to a soft purple as I worked my way across to the right of the painting. I left some of the Raw Sienna uncovered to represent the sun breaking through a diffused background. When the paint was approximately one-third dry, I painted the distant trees, using a stiffer mix of Payne's Gray/Permanent Sap Green to achieve a blurred effect to lead the viewer's eye into the distance.

The ivy on the trees was painted with a hog-hair brush using a stippling technique; dark tones of Burnt Umber/Permanent Sap Green were applied, followed by a paler, brighter green and finally white acrylic paint stippled on to give the effect of snow.

TREES AND SHADOWS

Using a rigger brush, the trunks and branches were initially painted with pale Raw Sienna. When the paint was approximately one-third dry, some dark tones of Burnt Umber were added to make the branches look realistic. The soft purple mix for the sky was also used to paint the shadows on the path, using the side of the round brush.

Snow

Using white acrylic paint is only one way of representing snow. There are other techniques – *see page 31.*

FOREGROUND TEXTURE

I lightly stippled a variety of colours using the edge of a hake brush, and left some white of the paper uncovered. I applied soft greens and Raw Sienna in the main and added a small amount of Payne's Gray for the darker tones. Finally, a little white has been stippled with a hog-hair brush to soften areas where the snow has drifted into the stubble.

ATMOSPHERE AND MOOD *Project*

1.

2.

In **Snow on the River** I'm going to show you a variety of watercolour techniques and how they can be combined to produce a successful painting.

1. MASKING AND POURING

After preparing the initial tonal study to establish the lights and darks and completing a simple drawing, I masked the tree shapes, the highlights I wanted to retain in the water and areas representing snow on the banks as well as areas of foliage.

Two washes were mixed in ceramic saucers, one using Cadmium Yellow Pale and one a mixture of Payne's Gray and Alizarin Crimson. The Cadmium Yellow mix was poured down the right-hand side of the painting and the Payne's Gray/Alizarin Crimson wash poured down the left-hand side. The board with the watercolour paper attached was inclined at a slight angle to allow the washes to flow down, blend together and run off the bottom of the paper.

2. PAINTING TREES

When the paint used in the first stage was dry, I painted the distant trees in light tones of Payne's Gray/Alizarin Crimson. Mixes of Raw Sienna and Burnt Sienna were applied to represent the bushes in the middle distance. I used the side of a size 14 round brush to paint the bushes. The fir trees were painted using a flat brush loaded with mixes of Permanent Sap Green and Payne's Gray.

3. REMOVING MASKING

Once the painting was completely dry, I removed the masking fluid by means of gentle rubbing with a putty eraser.

4. ADDING DETAILS

The tree shapes were painted with a rigger brush by applying a Raw Sienna wash over the trunks, followed by deposits of Burnt Umber to make them look natural. Using the sky colours, I painted shadows over the snow. The rocks were painted with a flat brush: Raw Sienna for their under-painting and Payne's Gray/Alizarin Crimson for the shadows under the rocks and in the water. To complete this stage, washes of Cadmium Yellow Pale, Raw Sienna and a weak Alizarin Crimson/Raw Sienna mix were painted over the white of the paper which had been restored after the removal of the masking from the trees and bushes.

The colours used

Payne's Gray — Alizarin Crimson — Raw Sienna — Burnt Umber — Cadmium Yellow Pale — Permanent Sap Green — Burnt Sienna

3.

4.

5. BALANCING TONE AND COLOUR

To complete this painting, I added a few more rocks in the river, painted darker tones of Payne's Gray/Alizarin Crimson underneath the trees and bushes and painted the foliage on the two young trees on the right-hand side. I also added several fir trees in the distance and a large boulder in the right foreground. Small amounts of white acrylic paint were applied to the trees to represent snow.

ATMOSPHERE, MOOD AND LIGHT *Useful Details*

We've already seen how useful it can be to include a feature in your painting other than what nature provides in the shape of the elements and the landscape. Many of the more common details are easy enough to paint. I'll show you how below.

SHEEP

When you come to paint sheep, think horseshoes. If the sheep is looking to the right, add a second horseshoe to extend the body to the right and then a triangle for the head. Naturally it is the same process only reversed if the animal is looking to the left – extending the body to the left and adding a triangle for its head. I use Payne's Gray/Burnt Umber to block in and then over-paint with either white acrylic paint or gouache. It's essential to add shadows beneath your sheep to make them look realistic.

FIGURES

So you think you can't paint figures? If you follow the steps shown, you'll find it easy. Before adding figures to your painting, it's a good idea to draw them first on clear film or tracing paper using a felt tip pen and then place this over your painting to determine the best position for them.

BOATS

Follow the simple stages shown and soon you will be competent to add boats to your paintings.

BUILDINGS

Here I have simplified the painting of a building. The dotted lines are included to help you simplify your drawing and show you how vanishing points go off into the distance. Linear perspective is the key to making your buildings look realistic.

To become a successful artist it's essential to understand tonal values, which I believe to be the most important contributing factor to painting a successful landscape.

All paintings need contrasts of tone and the balance between lights and darks arranged in relationships that enhance the quality of the painting. Many beginners tend to splash paint on without any preliminary thought about the design of their painting, and as a result what they produce looks flat and uninteresting.

It has always been my practice to clarify my thinking by producing small tonal sketches, using a dark brown water-soluble crayon. These sketches are only 3 x 4.5 inches in size and display little detail. Their purpose is to help me choose the best view of the landscape I am about to paint and to establish the best combination of light and darks. These tonal studies are simple scribbles but are vital to the success of my painting. If you produce tonal sketches to clarify your thinking before you apply paint, I guarantee that your paintings will improve significantly.

Utilizing Tonal Values

The following are two distinct ways in which tonal values can be successfully utilized in a painting, to ensure that your work never looks flat:

Counterchange is an effective way to highlight the principal subject matter in a painting, such as the focal point. By emphasizing lights against darks and darks against lights, interesting features can be made more distinctive. Examples could be: surrounding the light in a sky with darker contrasting tones of colour to make the light source appear brighter; painting a light toned figure against the dark background of a building; or painting dark trees behind the light toned roof of a building.

Gradation occurs when a colour gradually changes, either from a light tone to a darker tone or the reverse. Examples could be the transition in colour from foreground grass to that in the distance or the transition in colour from wet to dry sand on a beach.

Autumn Fields was painted on a warm, early autumn day. The focal point was the lone tree on the left. Darker tones were painted into this to make it more distinctive. Note the variation in tonal values in the grass areas, necessary to create realism in the scene. The distant trees were painted in lighter tones to achieve recession. The variety of colours and tones in the right-hand tree grouping gives structure and depth to the painting. The dark posts and bush on the left-hand bank serve to balance the larger tree grouping on the right.

How to transfer an outline drawing of a completed painting onto watercolour paper

The next technique is not a substitute for learning to draw and should only be used until you are competent at drawing.

1. Take a black and white photocopy of the painting to the size required.

2. Using a soft pencil (6B), scribble across the back of the photocopy.

3. Position the photocopy over your watercolour paper, trace around the outline and key features using a biro or 2H pencil.

4. Remove the photocopy. The image will have transferred to your paper ready for you to apply paint.

ATMOSPHERE, MOOD AND LIGHT *Close up*

Peace and Tranquillity depicts Scotland's salmon country. I was inspired by the atmospheric sky and the variety of tree species. The mountains provided the backcloth to the painting.

The only problem I encountered when painting this scene was presented by the many rocks in the river, which were time-consuming to paint.

I hope you enjoy painting this scene.

FIR TREES

Fir trees are quite easy to paint; simply use a flat brush and stipple, working upwards from ground level. As you stipple, rock the brush from side to side to define the shape, using more of the corner of the brush as you progress up each tree. Varying tones of Permanent Sap Green and Payne's Gray were used.

A number of bushes were painted in front of the fir trees to add variety of height, tone and colour. Some highlights were added to the foliage on the fir trees where the light reflected, using a mix of Cadmium Yellow and Permanent Sap Green with a little acrylic white added.

SKY AND MOUNTAINS

The sky is an important feature in this painting. The light from the sky softened the mountain structure and created sparkle on the surface of the water.

Skies such as this are easily painted. Apply the usual Raw Sienna wash, brush in the cloud shapes with, in this case, varying tones of blue and, to create the light effects, dab out some of the colour with a tissue to produce the feathery white clouds.

The mountains were painted with a hake brush, using sweeping directional strokes from peak to ground level. Shape your mountains by means of a tissue formed into a tight wedge, creating light areas by applying downward strokes at an approximate angle of 45° following the structure of the mountain. The colours used were Raw Sienna, Payne's Gray and Permanent Sap Green.

TREES, ROCKS AND RUNNING WATER

On the left bank were various young trees, their leaves changing colour as autumn approached. I stippled with a round hog-hair brush to create realistic looking foliage, using mixes made from Raw Sienna, Burnt Sienna, Permanent Sap Green and Payne's Gray.

When painting water it's a useful technique to partially close your eyes to allow observation of the various tones more clearly. A hake brush was used to paint the water, using Cerulean Blue/Payne's Gray mixes, taking care to leave lots of white paper uncovered to represent the light shimmering on the water.

A flat brush is ideal for shaping rocks. Paint a few of them at a time, applying a wash of Raw Sienna, followed by darker tones of Burnt Umber to give them shape. Don't forget to paint shadows under the rocks or they will look as if they are floating on the surface. This attention to detail distinguishes the more experienced painter from the beginner.

ATMOSPHERE, MOOD AND LIGHT *The seasons*

SPRING

It's spring, the new shoots are appearing, there's a fresh glow in the distance and the bluebells are in bloom. The birds are singing and everything in nature seems clean and new. Spring heralds the beginning of the artist's year.

When painting woodland scenes it's important to paint a simple sky that doesn't detract from the foreground detail. You must also design your painting so that the viewer's eye is taken beyond the foreground and into the distance. In this example I have used the path to lead the eye into the painting and out around the bend in the distance.

It's important to be able to paint a wide variety of greens. With four colours it's possible to mix over one hundred shades of green. For example, mix Payne's Gray and Raw Sienna together with varying quantities of water and you will create a range of very dark greens, olive greens and yellow greens. By mixing Cadmium Yellow Pale with Payne's Gray you will get a wide range of grass- and yellow-greens in dark and medium tones. Using Payne's Gray (the darkest blue) produces colours that are basically dark in tone, which makes them ideal for capturing shadows and depth.

In this painting a range of bright, sparkling greens was produced by experimenting with mixes of Cerulean Blue or French Ultramarine with Cadmium Yellow Pale. Cerulean Blue mixed with Raw Sienna will give yellow greens.

There are two techniques for painting bluebells. You can apply masking fluid, over-paint with greens, remove the masking and then paint over the white of the paper with French Ultramarine. Alternatively, you can paint the banks and when these are dry, over-paint with some white acrylic paint or gouache mixed with French Ultramarine. I chose the latter technique for this detail.

SUMMER

It's summertime and the tree structures can barely be seen due to the abundance of foliage. At ground level the grasses are in full growth and surrounding bushes are waiting for the young birds to leave their nests. The range of greens and siennas used to depict this woodland scene creates splashes of colour. The trees in full leaf cast shadows across the path, leading the eye into the distance.

Trees appear dark on the inside with light foliage sparkling on the outside. The water colourist paints light to dark, which conflicts with the previous statement and what is observed in nature.

My method when painting trees is to follow convention but after I have added darker tones to create depth, I will finish with touches of bright colour to soften the effect and create highlights.

Don't use black for shadows. Mix 20 per cent of any colour on your palette with 80 per cent Payne's Gray and you will produce an extensive range of blue, brown, red or green shadow colours that can be used where appropriate. My personal favourite for tree shadows is a mix of Payne's Gray with a small amount of Alizarin Crimson added.

To paint the grasses, I used a soft yellow green wash and stippled with darker tones of green using a hake and a hog-hair brush. I used a small natural sponge dipped in paint to stipple on the foliage. For the final highlights, I stippled with a round hog-hair brush once the under-painting had dried.

In this vignette, I used combinations of Cadmium Yellow Pale, Cerulean Blue, Raw Sienna, Burnt Umber and Payne's Gray.

127

ATMOSPHERE, MOOD AND LIGHT *The seasons*

AUTUMN

It is now autumn, my favourite time of year. The leaves have changed colour, and are now displaying a wonderful array of soft yellows to deep red-browns. Nature's colours are at their best at this time of year, and offer the landscape painter an abundance of majestic scenes to paint as well as opportunities to experiment with colour mixing.

As the trees change from their summer to autumn colours the woodland displays a great variety of soft greens, yellows, siennas, ochres and rich red-browns. Only touches of green are evident.

The less experienced painter will find the representation of foliage most difficult, whether they want to paint loosely or in great detail. In this painting the foliage was painted with a sponge, using a stippling technique.

The benefits of painting the same scene

Painting the same scene at different times of the year can be a fascinating and illuminating experience. It's both exciting and beneficial to your development as a landscape painter because it teaches you so much about colour mixing and gives you practice in a range of different techniques.

To paint this vignette, I mixed various colours from the selection of Cadmium Yellow Pale, Raw Sienna, Alizarin Crimson, Burnt Sienna, Burnt Umber and Payne's Gray.

WINTER

Winter has arrived. The leaves have fallen, except for a few determined to keep their lofty positions. The distant woodland appears diffused, yet the glory of what had been can still be seen in the occasional splash of colour. The ground is lightly covered in snow, with the young saplings and stubble projecting upwards.

Such a scene demands a simple background sky. In this example, a few downward strokes of a hake brush loaded with Cerulean Blue over a Raw Sienna under-painting sufficed. The painting will look too fussy if a complex sky is painted. Remember the 'Golden Rule': a detailed foreground demands a simple sky – a simple foreground requires an atmospheric sky.

The background trees were painted wet into wet, to create a diffused effect. This was achieved by using the corner of a hake brush, when the sky was approximately one-third dry. I scratched in the tree structures using a palette knife; a cocktail stick would also have done the job.

Timing is vital here. If the tree structures are to look almost white, the under-painting must not be too wet otherwise the paint will run back and you'll get dark tones. Experience will tell you when the time is right to begin scratching out.

This vignette shows the technique I used for painting the tree trunks. I defined the structure of the trees first by drawing them with a flat brush loaded with raw sienna. When the paint was approximately one-third dry, I removed some colour from the length of the trunk with a tissue shaped to a point. Finally, I used a rigger brush to paint some detail on the trunk using darker tones of Payne's Gray/Burnt Umber.

ATMOSPHERE, MOOD AND LIGHT *Techniques close up*

When writing these books, it was never my intention to attempt to impose a style of painting on anyone, but rather to show different techniques which would allow you to stamp your own style on your paintings with both confidence and pleasure. I like to think of an artist's style as being akin to handwriting in paint. You may wish to paint in a loose, free style or perhaps represent the landscape in detail. Over time you will develop your own style of painting – it can't be imposed on you.

Woodland Beck incorporates all the techniques described in this book. I used acrylic watercolours, but I could have used traditional watercolour paints just as easily.

FOLIAGE

After the tree structures were drawn in, the foliage was painted by initially stippling dark tones of a Payne's Gray/Permanent Sap Green mix. When this dark under-painting was dry, lighter greens were stippled over it. I used a round hog-hair brush (oil painter's brush) for this technique. The beauty of acrylics is that you can easily work light to dark or dark to light.

WATER

Initially I painted the fast-flowing water between the rocks. This was done by dipping the hairs of a round brush in Payne's Gray and then fanning them between thumb and finger to create irregular sections. The fine hairs were then quickly brushed between the rocks, which had the effect of leaving white paper uncovered to represent the running water.

I used a round, pointed brush with mixes of Payne's Gray and Cerulean Blue to add a variety of tones to complete the beck. The strokes were horizontal in direction. A little Raw Sienna was brushed in to represent reflections from the background light.

TEXTURE

There's considerable detailed texture in this painting to reflect the plant life you find when walking through woodland – tufts of grass, young bushes and saplings and, in this case, a carpet of bluebells.

Over the years, I have experimented with various brushes to achieve a natural look for depictions of a woodland floor. I find that stippling with an old oil painter's brush gives my preferred result, and I've used this method here.

ATMOSPHERE, MOOD AND LIGHT *Project*

Every artist dedicated to their work will be continually experimenting with new techniques to create paintings that stir their emotions. You might be fired to capture a sense of realism, the beauty of nature's creation or simply to complete a painting with which you are happy.

Experimentation is important if you want to be able to call on a wide range of techniques in your paintings. I have been able to produce several interesting landscapes by using different techniques, such as controlling the flow of paint with masking fluid or masking tape, pouring paint from saucers, scumbling, glazing, knifing out or spattering.

Autumn Flow is one such painting. I'm delighted to have the opportunity to show you some of the techniques I used to paint it.

1. MASKING AND POURING

An initial tonal study was completed and the outline of the painting drawn. Masking was applied by brush to the mountains and the water and to the foliage with a crumpled piece of grease-proof paper. A cocktail stick dipped in masking fluid was used to draw the tree structures.

The sky was painted with a hake brush loaded with mixes of Cerulean Blue and Alizarin Crimson and then allowed to dry.

The mountain was painted using a weak mixture of Payne's Gray and Alizarin Crimson and allowed to dry.

Washes of Raw Sienna, Burnt Sienna and Payne's Gray were pre-mixed in ceramic saucers and poured over the tree areas after the tops of the rocks had been masked out with a piece of masking tape to prevent the washes from running below this line. The board was tilted to allow the washes to run slowly and merge together. The paper was then laid flat to dry, with a hair dryer eventually used to ensure the paint was completely dry.

2. ESTABLISHING TONAL VALUES

Further pourings of the paint added depth to the trees. When this was dry the rough shapes of the fir trees were painted with a flat brush loaded with a Permanent Sap Green/Payne's Gray mix. The distant fir trees on the left were painted using a weaker mix.

3. REMOVING THE MASKING

The distant mountains were given more definition by applying a Payne's Gray/Alizarin Crimson wash. When this was dry a putty eraser was used to remove the masking from the mountains and the areas of foliage.

Painting the rocks is a very easy process, and comes next. Washes of Raw Sienna followed by Burnt Sienna and Payne's Gray are applied to selected areas. A palette knife is then used to shape the rocks. The paint isn't applied with the knife but simply moved around to create the shape of the rocks. At the end of each stroke of the knife, the build up of paint leaves a dark edge, representing shadows. The paper isn't damaged in any way by this.

Finally the masking was removed from the waterfall and the waterfall painted in a Payne's Gray/Cerulean Blue mix using light strokes with a hake brush following the direction of flow. The rocks projecting through the water were painted using a flat brush loaded with the colours used previously.

4. ADDING DETAIL

It's time to bring the painting together and add the finishing touches. Raw Sienna, Cadmium Yellow Pale and Burnt Sienna glazes were applied to the foliage and tree structures. These same glazes were also used to colour the rocks and create depth of tone.

Highlights to the foliage were then applied. Paper masks had to be first cut to shape to protect other areas, such as the sky; I used a piece of mounting card cut to various profiles to fit around the trees. To apply the paint, I took an old toothbrush, dipped it in Cadmium Yellow Pale, ran my thumb over the bristles and then spattered the colour onto the foliage.

Taking time to get it right

I rarely complete a painting in one sitting. I prefer to work on it over several days, looking at it critically and making any changes I feel are necessary. I might remove paint to lighten areas or apply glazes (a little paint mixed with lots of water) to improve the variation of colour and tone.

Using the above process, I have been able to produce several interesting landscapes and enjoy this different approach to painting. I recommend you try these methods – above all, have fun and enjoy your painting.

The colours used

Payne's Gray

Alizarin Crimson

Raw Sienna

Cerulean Blue

Cadmium Yellow Pale

Permanent Sap Green

Burnt Sienna

133

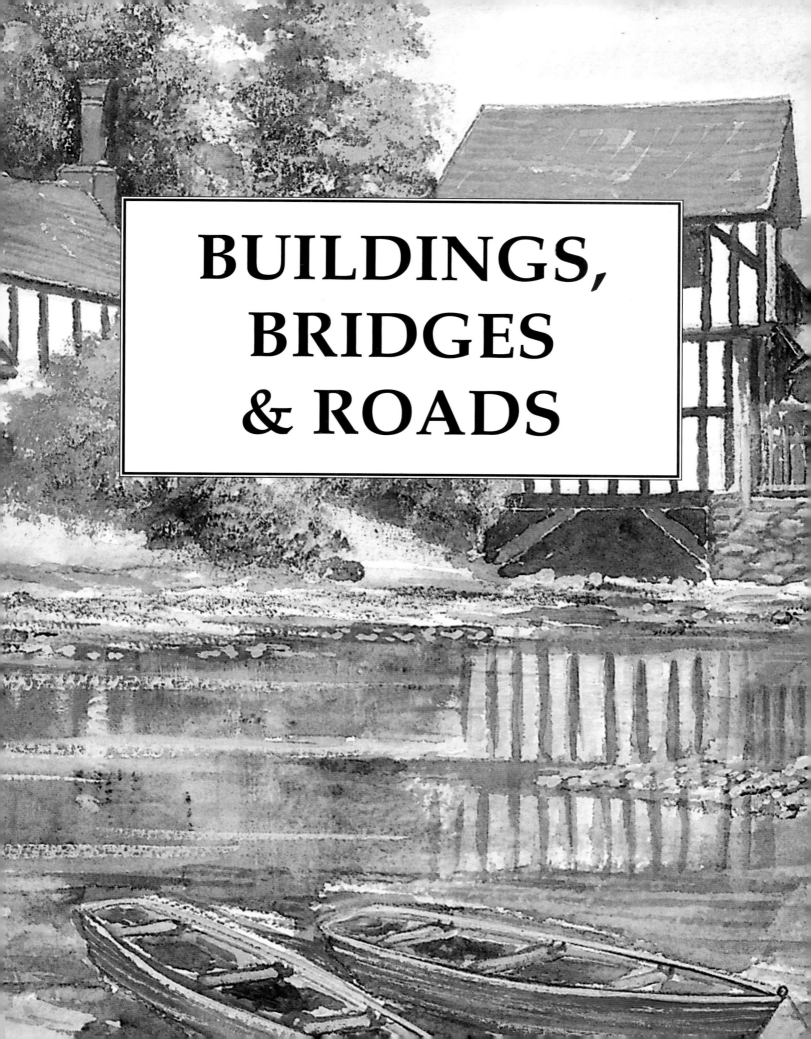

BUILDINGS, BRIDGES & ROADS

PAINTING BUILDINGS *Introduction*

The subject of buildings covers a very wide field. Because they come in a variety of shapes and forms, buildings offer the watercolourist an exciting range of opportunities. In this book, I have attempted to reflect this range by showing you my approach to painting many different types of building, from old farmsteads to medieval castles.

I am fascinated by the structure of buildings and the textures you find in them. An interesting window, an old door with rusty hinges, a stairway or an element in a street scene with people, all are worthwhile subjects. You don't have to paint a complete landscape to get a rewarding watercolour.

To paint buildings well, it's important to be able to sketch and draw reasonably accurately to represent the scene effectively. I felt it was necessary, therefore, to include in the text some basic instruction on how to draw. Drawing isn't difficult, just common sense, but there's an approach to drawing that I follow, which I will explain in the following pages.

Perspective plays an important part in drawing buildings. Some people find perspective easy, other people don't. Fortunately, I have never experienced problems with it. If you do, don't worry. I intend to simplify perspective for you later in the book.

Paintings don't just happen, they have to be designed. And if you learn how to do this your end result won't be just a matter of luck. You will discover that you must establish a plan using your imagination, asking yourself what the main features in your chosen picture are and how you can emphasize them. Tonal values, colour, texture and contrast all play a part in this. In the exercises and demonstrations in this section, I will be describing and showing how all this is done.

Payne's Gray

Cobalt Blue

Alizarin Crimson

Vermilion

Raw Sienna

Burnt Sienna

Burnt Umber

Majestic **Durham Cathedral***, overlooking the River Wear in the north of England, makes a lovely scene to paint.*

Fountains Abbey in Yorkshire. When I painted this scene the sun was shining on the abbey, throwing it into stark relief against the heavy shadows in the trees and across the path.

Practice

- *Study the examples in this book and practise painting wet into wet skies to represent the various light situations.*
- *Practise colour mixing, using the colours specified in the text.*
- *Practise using an eraser to remove colour, creating shafts of light as in a woodland glade or an atmospheric sky.*

BUILDINGS, BRIDGES and WALLS *Sketching on location*

There's no substitute for sketching and drawing. No matter how good you are at applying paint, if your initial drawing is out of scale and your perspective is wrong the end result will be a failure. Draw, draw and more drawing is the answer.

The sketches I produce when on location are not intended to be masterclass drawings but quick doodles to act as a record of my visit to an area or as a simple outline direct on to watercolour paper ready for applying paint at a later date. The amount of detail you include in your sketches or outline drawings and the techniques you use to create texture will depend on the particular subject, the time available for drawing or the intended use of the finished work. Knowing when to stop will come with experience.

Sketching and drawing is a pleasant relaxing experience which forces you to think about your subject and observe it very closely. When you have been sketching and drawing for some time you will no longer think about your style but concentrate on the statement you are trying to make.

Windmills near Amsterdam.

Windmills of Amsterdam

Drawing Materials

How you interpret your subject is personal, whether you use pencil, crayon, charcoal, conté crayon, felt tip pen or drawing pen and ink. My personal choice includes 4B and 6B pencils, water-soluble crayons or drawing pens (sizes 0.5 and 0.7mm). For both pencil and pen work, I like to use 2 ply Bristol board which has a bright white surface. When using water-soluble crayons, I find the fine texture of an oil or acrylic painting pad is perfect for creating shading and textures speedily.

Approaches to Sketching

I find many of my students just want to paint and ruin a perfectly good piece of watercolour paper without spending the time observing their subject, simplifying the scene, studying the relationships of darks and lights, the direction of light and shadows and the scale of the various elements in the scene.

The time spent drawing provides you with thinking time, the opportunity to produce several sketches to help establish the best viewing point to determine the best composition. Try to spend three minutes observing and thinking to every minute drawing or painting.

Use of a Viewfinder

We all have our likes and dislikes – what we sketch is that which appeals to us and how we feel about the subject at the time. A viewfinder can help us to select what appeals to us. It is useful for identifying potential scenes from different viewpoints, and helps to establish the best composition. It's very easy to make your own viewfinder which you can cut from a piece of mounting card. The one I use has an aperture of 4½in x 3in.

When you view a scene, get into the habit of looking at what's before your eyes in terms of the lines, colours, textures, tonal values, shapes and contrasts they present. Don't think of what is there as being buildings, trees, mountains, or whatever it happens to be. That approach will only limit your imagination.

Quick Sketching

When visiting an area I produce quick sketches, supplemented by photographs, from which I can produce a completed painting on my return to my studio. Sketching and drawing on location with limited time sharpens your observation of the scene. It encourages you to simplify, discarding unnecessary detail that doesn't contribute significantly to the overall representation.

Squinting one's eyes to view the subject helps to establish the lights and darks, eliminating unnecessary detail. As an artist you must create your own composition using your imagination and skills to simplify and organize your subject in accordance with the principles of good design.

The poet Wordsworth's home at Grasmere in the English Lake District.

A view of the medieval city of Bruges.

The initial black and white sketch or drawing is an important aspect of planning before you begin applying watercolour. Through your tonal studies you can determine the most attractive composition and work out your values and shapes. Use artistic licence, if necessary, to improve your composition. Simplify and prepare your drawing loosely or in detail. I personally prefer to draw on to my watercolour paper with a dark brown water-soluble crayon because I do not like to see pencil marks in a finished painting. When I draw faintly with the crayon and apply my watercolour washes, the lines will wash out.

Both sketches were drawn with a drawing pen and shaded with a water-soluble crayon.

Drawing a Street Scene

For this street scene, follow the same procedure as that given for drawing the Grand Canal opposite. Take particular care getting the perspective of the roofs, footpaths and windows right. Each block of buildings has a different vanishing point.

Getting the size right

Drawing isn't difficult providing you follow a logical procedure. When drawing a complex scene, where a significant number of buildings is involved, always use a piece of watercolour paper that is larger than is actually required.

Draw in your buildings and then trim your painting to size. There's nothing more frustrating than starting your drawing and running out of paper before you've drawn all of the buildings. Using a larger sheet and trimming to size until you've mastered the art of drawing to scale will avoid the frustration of having to rub out and virtually begin again.

Drawing the Grand Canal, Venice

When drawing any group of buildings, there's a logical procedure I follow. If you adopt this approach you will be able to draw most scenes realistically. The procedure:

• Commence by establishing the angles of the water levels and the vanishing point.

• Draw one building in the scene first, making sure the height of the building is in proportion to its frontage.

• Draw in the vertical lines of all other buildings, taking care that the length of frontage of each building is in proportion to that of the adjoining buildings.

• Draw in the height of each building in proportion to its frontage and the height of its neighbours.

• Hold your pen or pencil at arm's length and line it up with the angle of the roof, moving your arm downtowards your paper to determine the correct linear perspective.

• Finally, draw in the windows, steps, balconies, etc.

It's as easy as that. Following this logical procedure will ensure that your buildings are drawn to scale in the correct proportions. If your buildings are out of proportion and your perspective is incorrect, no matter how good you are at applying paint the result won't be pleasing.

PAINTING BUILDINGS *Project*

Under a Norfolk Sky provided me with the opportunity to show how to paint an atmospheric sky and to include a windmill, one of many to be discovered in this eastern region of England. This is a very simple exercise for you to try. For the painting to work the atmospheric sky is essential.

1. SKY

I used a water-soluble crayon to draw the windmill, buildings and riverbank. The sky was painted using a 1½ in hake brush by initially wetting the paper with a very pale Raw Sienna and brushing in the dark clouds using mixes made from Cerulean Blue, Payne's Gray, and Burnt Sienna.

Circular movements of the brush were used to create the impression of cumulus clouds, working around light areas. Larger clouds were created at the top of the painting and smaller clouds approaching the horizon to achieve linear perspective.

The same colours used for the sky were used to paint the water.

2. WINDMILL

The windmill tower was painted by initially applying a Raw Sienna wash and whilst still wet brushing in some Burnt Sienna and a Payne's Gray/Cerulean Blue mix, allowing the colours to spread and blend together.

The red roofs of the buildings were painted with a ¾ in flat brush loaded with a mixture of approximately 20 per cent Alizarin Crimson and 80 per cent Burnt Sienna. The brickwork at the base of the windmill and the door were painted using this same mix. The walls of the buildings were painted using the same colours and techniques used to paint the windmill tower.

Finally the windmill blades and safety fencing were painted using a rigger brush, and the grass painted using a variety of greens.

3. TREES

It's time to paint the trees and bushes using a mixture of greens made from Cadmium Yellow Pale, Raw Sienna, Permanent Sap Green and Payne's Gray. A round hog-hair oil painter's brush was used to stipple in the foliage, taking care to ensure a variety of tree shapes and heights. I used a palette knife to scratch in some tree structures. Some darker tones were used to emphasize the edge of the riverbank.

Payne's Gray	Alizarin Crimson	Raw Sienna	Cerulean Blue

Cadmium Yellow Pale	Permanent Sap Green	Burnt Sienna

4. REFLECTIONS AND FOREGROUND

It's time to bring the painting together and add the finishing touches. Raw Sienna, Cadmium Yellow Pale and Burnt Sienna glazes were applied to the foliage and tree structures. These same glazes were also used to colour the rocks and create depth of tone.

Highlights to the foliage were then applied. Paper masks had to be first cut to shape to protect other areas, such as the sky; I used a piece of mounting card cut to various profiles to fit around the trees. To apply the paint, I took an old toothbrush, dipped it in Cadmium Yellow Pale, ran my thumb over the bristles and then spattered the colour onto the foliage.

BUILDINGS, BRIDGES and WALLS *Linear perspective*

When drawing buildings, perspective is an important consideration if you want to make your drawing look believable. Most of my students find perspective difficult. Let's see if we can simplify the subject.

Where your eye meets the horizon is called the eye level. This imaginary line is a straight horizontal line which will naturally change as you lower or elevate your viewpoint.

In the first diagram we are looking straight at our subject from a viewpoint slightly to the left, enabling us to see the gable end of the building. The lines of the roof, windows and ground level converge to one point on the right; this is known as the 'vanishing point'. Because we can see the end of the building, all lines will converge to a vanishing point on the horizon line to the left; this is known as two-point perspective.

In the second diagram we are looking down at our subject. Our eye level is higher than the building. The same principles apply, though.

When painting outdoors all you have to do is hold a pen or pencil directly in front of you and line it up with the top of the roof. Move your arm down to your paper and draw in the angle. Repeat this process with other parts of the building to establish the correct perspective.

An even simpler technique is to cut yourself an aperture from a piece of mounting card and position some elastic bands around the perimeter. View your subject through the viewfinder. Line up the elastic bands with various elements of the building (ie. roof, windows, base, etc.) and, transferring this to your paper, draw along the elastic bands to ensure the correct linear perspective.

144

Note the perspective in this quick sketch of the old village of **Beget in the Pyrenees**. The angles at the top of the tower in particular are good examples of linear perspective.

Beget in the Pyrenees
Keith Fenwick

This sketch of **The Creek near Salcombe** in Devon, England was a lovely scene to draw and paint. My students found the perspective quite challenging. The roofs of the thatched cottages highlight the need for the perspective to be correct if the sketch is going to work.

The Creek - NR Salcombe, Devon 2002

145

BUILDINGS, BRIDGES and WALLS *Creating textures*

One of the beauties of watercolour is its transparency, making it an ideal medium to create textures on buildings. Buildings come in many shapes and sizes and offer the artist numerous exciting features to paint. The rough texture of stonework, the watermarks, cracks, crumbling plaster and weathered exteriors can all make fascinating subjects to capture in watercolour, using a limited range of colours.

The texture on the stonework surrounding this window in Brittany was painted by initially applying white and dark brown oil pastels to areas of white paper. A Raw Sienna wash was applied to the whole of the stonework and while it was still wet, Burnt Sienna and a Payne's Gray/Alizarin Crimson mixture was selectively applied to the stonework. The deposits of oil pastel repelled the watercolour washes, creating the textured effect. Finally, the shadows around the individual stones were emphasized using various tones of Payne's Gray.

Window in Morbihan - Brittany

Image of Provence

I have attempted to capture the weathered exterior of this old apartment in Provence by initially wetting the paper with a pale Raw Sienna wash and while this was still wet dropping in some Burnt Sienna and a Payne's Gray/Cobalt Blue mixture. The colours have been allowed to blend together wet into wet. A size 6 brush used to move colour to create the effect of weathering.

Round chimney - the sign of an old building - note the dovecote

I was fascinated with this old building in the English Lake District. The round chimney signifies its age. Note too the dovecote at the base of the chimney, leading in to the roof area. The originally brick building was painted white and weathering had created some surface stains. I applied a weak Cobalt Blue wash to selected areas and when this was dry I indicated brickwork using a rigger brush loaded with a Payne's Gray/Cobalt Blue mix. Note how the bricks on the chimney were drawn at a slight curve to indicate the round chimney.

The dormer window, which fits into the roof, is a subject often drawn incorrectly.

Victorian Postbox at Wasdale Head

I couldn't resist painting this old Victorian postbox housed in a rough stonewall in the hamlet of Wasdale in the English Lake District. The postbox was painted using various tones of an Alizarin Crimson/Vermilion mix to look realistic.

The texture on the stonework was achieved by initially drawing the outlines of the stones and making deposits with both white and cream oil pastels. A Raw Sienna wash was applied overall and splashes of Burnt Sienna and a mix of Payne's Gray/Alizarin Crimson applied wet into wet. An absorbent tissue was used to lighten the stonework by dabbing to remove paint. The shadows around the stones were painted in last. The oil pastel repelled the watercolour paint, resulting in a weathered textured appearance.

147

BUILDINGS, BRIDGES and WALLS *Colour mixing and tonal value*

Colour is a continuous source of fascination to artists. Colour and light are what we first see when we look at the landscape. When painting buildings, I use few colours, finding that I am able to capture most building structures using a limited palette consisting of Raw Sienna, Burnt Sienna, Burnt Umber for stonework,

supported by Payne's Gray, Alizarin Crimson and Cobalt Blue for shadows, watermarks, weathered plaster, etc., and for brickwork, I may introduce Vermilion. The blues I find useful are Cobalt Blue, French Ultramarine or Cerulean Blue, depending on the light.

Raw Sienna

Burnt Sienna

Burnt Umber

Payne's Gray/Alizarin Crimson

Cobalt Blue/Alizarin Crimson

Vermilion/French Ultramarine

Check List

• *Produce tonal studies to establish the best viewpoint and to determine the relationship between the lights and darks.*

• *Don't forget to get your perspective correct or your buildings won't look right.*

• *Don't include elements in your paintings that aren't characteristic of the region*

• *Great designers simplify and eliminate.*

In **Early Morning on the Lake** *the background is diffused with little detail. The boat in the foreground was included to balance the grouping of dark trees on the left of the painting.*

It has always been my practice to produce simple sketches or tonal value studies to determine the ideal viewpoint giving the most pleasing composition. These are simple 'doodles' produced in a few minutes and showing little detail. Approximately 3in x 2in in size, they help me think about my approach to the painting prior to applying paint.

They are my plan of action, helping me to establish the dominant tonal values and the areas of greatest contrast. They help me to plan my approach to the painting, encouraging me to observe and simplify. I use a dark brown water-soluble crayon to produce my tonal studies. I cannot over emphasize the importance of establishing the relationships between the lights and darks in a painting.

The subject here, **Lakeland Farm at Mungrisdale**, *is backlit. Note the darker tones on the stonework which is in shadow.*

EXERCISES

• Work through the demonstrations until you feel confident to produce your own compositions.
• Travel with a sketch book and produce as many drawings as it takes for you to draw buildings easily.
• Study lots of buildings – note the angles of roofs and their structural lines and practise drawing them until you

have mastered the principles of linear perspective and can produce realistic drawings incorporating them.
• Select an interesting dormer window. Note how it fits into the roof.
• Choose a weathered wall or unusual doorway and sketch and paint its features.

PAINTING BUILDINGS *Close up*

Cape Town's famous waterfront, with its restaurants, shopping mall, bustling harbour and magnificent Table Mountain as a backdrop, was irresistible as a subject for painting while I was on a recent trip to South Africa. I painted the scene shown here later in my studio from sketches and photographs taken from a boat at sea.

SKY AND MOUNTAIN

The simple sky was painted with a mix of Cobalt and Cerulean Blue. Darker washes were applied top left to provide some gradation of colour. A tissue was used to remove paint, indicating a few wispy white clouds. Table Mountain was painted by applying various tones of a Payne's Gray/Cerulean Blue mix over a Raw Sienna under-painting and creating highlights with a tissue shaped to a chisel edge.

BUILDINGS

The buildings were drawn in lightly with a 4B pencil and masking fluid applied to windows, doors, balconies, parasols and boats. When dry various washes of Raw Sienna and Payne's Gray were applied. When these washes were dry, the masking was removed and the parasols and boats painted.

Perspective

Spend some time drawing to scale to enable you to get the proportions of each building right. Ensure your perspective is reasonably accurate, otherwise your finished painting will be a failure.

150

WATER AND DETAILS

Masking was initially applied to the water to represent light reflections. When the masking was dry, washes of Raw Sienna, Payne's Gray and Cerulean Blue were applied. The masking was removed when the paint was dry, and then a pale wash of Raw Sienna applied.

Finally figures were painted and the canopies coloured blue and green.

PAINTING BUILDINGS *Project*

The Grand Canal in Venice has been a favourite of artists over many generations. The most time-consuming aspect of this painting was the initial drawing of the buildings which I had to ensure were in proportion to one another. The many windows were also a challenge. I used the procedure outlined on page 12 to draw the scene.

1. PREPARATORY DRAWING AND SKY

The waterline was drawn in followed by the verticals of the building, ensuring that the length of frontage of each building was in proportion to that of its neighbour. The height of each building was established in proportion to its frontage. The windows, balconies, canopies and parasols were drawn and masking fluid applied to maintain the white of the paper. Masking was also selectively applied to areas of the water.

The sky was painted using Payne's Gray, Raw Sienna, Alizarin Crimson and French Ultramarine. The same colours were used to paint the water as a mirror image.

2. BUILDINGS

Artistic licence was used to create warmer colours in the buildings than was apparent. Mixtures of Raw Sienna, Burnt Sienna and Alizarin Crimson were washed over the buildings, using a hake brush. Cobalt Blue was then dropped in here and there to indicate weathering. A Payne's Gray/Alizarin Crimson mix was used to paint in the shadows.

3. WINDOWS AND DETAILS

The roofs were painted using an Alizarin Crimson/Burnt Sienna mix. The windows were painted by applying various tones of a Payne's Gray/Alizarin Crimson mix. While the paint was still wet, a tissue shaped to a point was used to dab the windows, removing paint to suggest reflections of light. The same mixture was painted over the balconies. When this was dry the masking was removed, leaving white areas around the balconies and the windows. Next the masking was removed from the parasols and canopies prior to applying paint. The masking in the water was not removed at this stage.

The colours used

Payne's Gray	Alizarin Crimson	Raw Sienna	Cobalt Blue	French Ultramarine	Permanent Sap Green	Burnt Sienna

4. GONDOLAS

Before painting the gondolas I established their best positions by initially drawing their shapes with a felt-tip pen (water-based non-permanent) on a clear acetate sheet and then moving this over the water. Finally, the mooring posts were painted in.

5. WATER

The water was over-painted using a hake brush loaded with mixtures of Payne's Gray, Cobalt Blue and Permanent Sap Green. When the paint was dry the masking was removed using a putty eraser.

PAINTING BUILDINGS *Close up*

I have painted this boathouse many times. Located on the shores of Lake Ullswater, in the English Lake District, it's a special place where I have spent many enjoyable hours. It's a very peaceful place to sit and paint. My favourite time is in the evening when the tourists have retired for their evening meal and I am left with a few swans or ducks for company. Acrylic watercolours were used for this painting, which was done for a TV programme.

After painting the sky and mountains, I painted the trees, boathouse and shore, leaving the water until last.

SKY

The sky was a feature in this painting. Using acrylic watercolours, I used a Raw Sienna wash and then, with a hake, brushed in Payne's Gray and Burnt Umber. When this was dry, I created the white edges to the clouds by wiggling the side of a size 14 round brush dipped in Titanium White.

MOUNTAINS AND WATER

The mountains were brushed in with a hake brush after a piece of masking tape had been positioned across the painting to represent the waterline. Raw Sienna and Burnt Umber mixes were used and the row of distant trees was painted by adding a little Permanent Sap Green to the mixture. The masking tape was removed when the paint was dry.

Horizontal strokes with the side of the size 14 round brush were used to paint the reflections in the water over an initial Raw Sienna under-painting while this was still wet. A Payne's Gray/Cerulean Blue mix was brushed in to create variety in the water. The swans were painted last.

154

trying to make and complete your painting with the minimum number of brush strokes.

TREES

The trees were painted by initially applying a Burnt Umber under-painting around the drawing of the boathouse. Then I stippled a range of greens, using an old bristle brush, to create the impression of foliage.

BOATHOUSE

The stonework on the boathouse and access ramp was completed by applying a Raw Sienna wash and dropping in Burnt Sienna and Burnt Umber wet into wet. When this was dry, a rigger loaded with Titanium White was used to create the effect of mortar around individual stones. The balcony entrance and landing stage were then painted. Don't forget the fence in the middle distance; I painted this using a fine rigger brush. I used the same brush for the smoke from the chimney, painted in white over a Payne's Gray under-painting.

PAINTING BUILDINGS *Project*

I could not resist painting this beautiful Tuscan villa in watercolour. Constructed on a hilltop with magnificent views over the surrounding countryside and having many pleasing design features, it is one of the most impressive villas I have come across. I thought it would make an excellent exercise for a painting project.

I used artistic license to improve the composition, by adding the groups of trees. A 4B pencil was used to carefully make the outline drawing.

1. SKY

The simple sky was painted with a 1½ in hake brush. Graduated washes of Cerulean Blue were applied – darker tones at the top, becoming progressively paler as I worked downwards and added more water to weaken the mixture. The wispy white clouds were created by removing paint with a soft tissue using a dabbing action.

2. BUILDINGS

To represent the stonework, an initial weak Raw Sienna wash was applied using a ¾ in flat brush. I concentrated on one section at a time and while the wash was still wet brushed in some Burnt Sienna and a little Cerulean Blue, allowing the colours to blend together with the wet under-painting. When the paint was completely dry, I brushed in indications of stonework using a size 6 round brush.

The other half of the building was painted in the same way. The roofs were painted using a mix of approximately 20 per cent Alizarin Crimson and 80 per cent Burnt Sienna.

3. ADDING DETAILS

The next stage was to paint the windows and doors. For the windows, I used a size 6 brush loaded with a mix of Payne's Gray/Alizarin Crimson. While the paint was still wet, I dabbed at it with a tissue rolled to a point to remove colour. This technique absorbed paint, creating the atmospheric effect of light reflecting off the glass.

The doors were painted using a mix of Burnt Umber/Burnt Sienna. When this mixture was dry, I took a rigger brush loaded with Burnt Umber and using downward stokes represented the planks of wood that made up the doors. A soft green was brushed in to indicate vegetation at the base of the villa and a few plants growing in the terracotta pots.

4. FINAL TOUCHES

The foreground grass was painted using a hake brush loaded with a variety of soft greens in varying tones, made from mixes of Cadmium Yellow Pale, Raw Sienna and Payne's Gray. When the paint was dry, I painted the path leading from the foreground to the villa using mixes of Raw Sienna /Burnt Umber.

Finally the trees were painted by stippling in mixes of Cerulean Blue and Permanent Sap Green with a ³/₄ in flat brush. Payne's Gray was added to the trees in the immediate foreground to give them dark tones.

The colours used

| Payne's Gray | Burnt Umber | Raw Sienna | Cerulean Blue | French Ultramarine | Permanent Sap Green | Burnt Sienna |

PAINTING BUILDINGS *Close up*

The 14th-century manor house at Lower Brockhampton, now owned by the National Trust, is a lovely old timbered building, with a detailed 15th-century gatehouse straddling the moat. I have included this scene as an exercise in drawing because it makes a pleasing composition and is useful practice for drawing and perspective. It's important to ensure the buildings are drawn in proportion and the perspective is accurate. Study the angles of the roofs and try to represent them accurately.

SKY
Remember the Golden Rule: a detailed foreground demands a simple sky. With this in mind a simple wet into wet sky was painted using Payne's Gray, Cerulean Blue over a Raw Sienna under-painting. A tissue was used to shape the cloud structures. The sky was painted using my 1½ in hake brush.

WATER AND FOLIAGE
The water was as usual painted in last using mixes of Payne's Gray, Cerulean Blue and Permanent Sap Green. Note the reflections from the trees and buildings. It's not necessary to paint a complete mirror image of the buildings, just include a few of the main factors to indicate reflections. Impressions of a few water-lilies were included. Note the variation in the foliage of the bushes and trees. An old bristle brush was used to create light areas of foliage and flowers on the bushes near the building, using a stippling action. To paint the lighter foliage, add a little white acrylic or gouache to your watercolour paints. If you do this the detail will stay on top of the under-painting, whereas traditional watercolour on its own will sink into the under-painting.

Checklist

• When painting buildings you will need to sit well back in order to fit in the number of buildings necessary to obtain a good composition.

• Never paint a building front on. You will need to sit slightly to one side to see some of the gable end. It makes a much more pleasing composition.

• Make sure you draw the perspective correctly or your painting won't look realistic.

• Squint your eyes when viewing – it helps to establish the light and dark tones and eliminate unnecessary detail.

BUILDINGS AND BANKS

A Burnt Sienna/Alizarin Crimson mix was used to paint the roofs, chimneys and brickwork. The extensive woodwork was painted using a Payne's Gray/Burnt Umber mix. Take care to ensure your perspective is correct. The windows were painted by applying a Payne's Gray/Alizarin Crimson mix and dabbing with a tissue to soften areas. To achieve gradation in the grass banks, I applied a weak Raw Sienna wash and brushed in a mid-green to selected areas, followed by darker green, brushing upwards from the water's edge. The colours will blend together, achieving a subtle gradation in the greens. If you over-do it, use a tissue shaped to a wedge to lift colour to create lighter areas.

PAINTING BUILDINGS *Project*

The old mill at Langstone in Hampshire, England was once a famous spot for landing contraband. It is now a peaceful haven for bird watchers and sailing enthusiasts. I think you will enjoy painting this scene.

1. SKY
Care was taken to ensure the drawing was in correct linear perspective and each building was in proportion to its neighbour in terms of height, width and length. I commenced by drawing the right-hand group of buildings, making sure the mill tower was correct in diameter and height in relation to the building.

Masking fluid was applied to the windows, the railing and to highlight reflections and other areas in the water. The sailor and boat were also masked.

The sky was painted using a 1½ in hake brush and various mixes of Payne's Gray, Cerulean Blue and Alizarin Crimson over a Raw Sienna under-painting. Brush strokes were directed towards the mill tower. The same colours were used to paint the water.

2. BUILDINGS
A Payne's Gray/Burnt Sienna mix was applied to the mill tower and the dark areas at water level. A Payne's Gray/Cerulean Blue mix was used to over-paint the masking on the railings, the front of the pavilion and windows.

Approximately 20 per cent Alizarin Crimson and 80 per cent Burnt Sienna were used to mix a rich reddish brown colour for the roofs. The stonework was painted by initially applying a weak Raw Sienna and while this was still wet dabbing in some Burnt Sienna and Cerulean Blue, allowing the paint variations to blend together.

3. TREES AND WATER
The trees in the distance and middle distance were painted using a variety of light and dark greens made from mixes of Raw Sienna and Permanent Sap Green.

More depth was created in the water by applying various darker tones of a Payne's Gray/Cerulean Blue mixture, painting over the masking, which repelled the various washes. The brickwork supports were painted and using the same mix (Raw Sienna, Burnt Sienna, Alizarin Crimson) some reflections were painted in the water.

4. ADDING DETAIL

The boat was painted after removing the masking with a putty eraser and the sailor added using the rigger brush loaded with dark green. A few posts and the landing stage were painted on the far left using a Payne's Gray/Burnt Umber mix. Highlights were added to the water using a white water-soluble crayon.

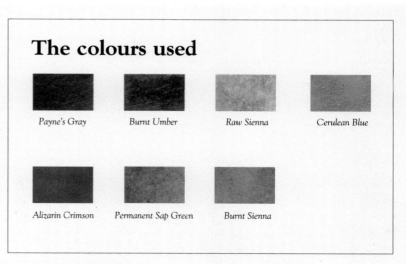

The colours used

Payne's Gray	Burnt Umber	Raw Sienna	Cerulean Blue
Alizarin Crimson	Permanent Sap Green	Burnt Sienna	

PAINTING BUILDINGS *Close up*

Portsoy Harbour, on the north-east coast of Scotland, is a favourite location of mine, and frequently used by me and my students during painting holidays. There are myriad painting opportunities here.

When painting stonework, you have to use artistic licence to provide colour and variation to the buildings. If they are all a dull brown your painting will look drab and lack interest, so don't be afraid to drop in a few warm colours here and there.

SKY

Remember the Golden Rule: a detailed foreground demands a simple sky; a simple foreground demands an atmospheric sky. In this painting the sky had to be simple because there is so much detail. I applied a Raw Sienna under-painting and while this was less than one-third dry painted in the clouds with Cobalt/Cerulean Blue. A few white clouds were formed using a tissue.

HARBOUR WALL

This part of the composition was simply painted by applying a Raw Sienna wash and brushing in a Payne's Gray/Alizarin Crimson mix to add darker tones. The effect of stonework in the wall in the foreground was created by moving paint with a palette knife – a very simple but effective technique. Using a softened white water-soluble crayon, a few highlights were created. Finally the fishing boat was painted.

Proportion

When painting buildings spend some time drawing them in proportion relative to each other. The simple stages to follow are shown on pages 12 and 13.

BUILDINGS, WATER AND DETAILS

To achieve variation in the stonework, Raw Sienna washes were initially applied. While these were still wet, Burnt Sienna and a Payne's Gray/Alizarin Crimson mix were brushed in to selected areas. There wasn't much reflected variation in the windows on this occasion.

The water in the harbour was painted with a mix of Permanent Sap Green and Payne's Gray using horizontal strokes applied with the side of a size 14 round brush. There were many visitors to the harbour on the day I was there, and so I added some figures to give life to my painting.

BRIDGES and WALLS *Introduction*

Bridges and walls are functional creations. Bridges are usually built to span a river or canyon, whereas walls mark out areas of land, such as fields and pastures, or the limits of somebody's territory. Bridges come in all shapes and sizes, in a variety of materials, from cut stone and brick to wood, concrete or iron. Generally speaking, walls and bridges made out of modern materials offer far fewer challenges to the artist, and it is for this reason I have concentrated on showing you examples made out of traditional materials such as stone. Many of these are works of art in their design, especially the stone bridges and walls found in country districts, where the traditions that go into their building are often closely associated.

Traditional bridges and walls offer artists wonderful opportunities to exercise their skills. Quite apart from their sheer beauty, they are master works of design and craftsmanship. Over the years I have derived immense pleasure from painting them. I hope you too will be rewarded by seeing the workmanship and ingenuity that has gone into their construction.

In the following pages, I'm going to show you some helpful techniques and give you opportunities to practise them. The colours I find most useful when painting bridges and walls are shown below.

Wades Bridge is an unusual shaped bridge in Scotland. Almost a perfect semi-circle, it is a mystery why it needed to be built so high. This uncharacteristic shape in what is a picturesque setting inspired me to paint this scene.

The colours used

| Payne's Gray | Burnt Umber | Raw Sienna | Cobalt Blue | Alizarin Crimson | Burnt Sienna |

Fine examples of a bridge and walls can be found at Longsleddale in the English Lake District.

Points to remember

- The structure is the starting point for any successful painting of a bridge or wall.
- Look for the small details that make each wall different. 'Hogg' holes, for example, are holes which allow yearling sheep, called 'hoggs', to pass through the wall to reach further grazing areas. Postboxes are often incorporated into a stone wall, and stone gateposts have holes which allow poles to be positioned across an opening instead of a gate. 'Rabbit snoops' for catching rabbits are built into some walls. Many ingenious practical devices are incorporated in stone walls. Look out for them.
- Each waller will use the type of stones available to him in the vicinity. As artists, we need to take this into account when painting stonework. If the walls are near a river the stones may be round, if near a quarry long and thin, so paint your wall accordingly.
- When painting bridges, try to select a viewpoint which enables some of the underneath of the arches to be seen. This makes a more pleasing composition.
- When incorporating stone walls in your composition, never paint them stretching from one side of your painting to the other without leaving an opening or incorporating a gate. Otherwise you are putting up barriers to the viewer and saying, 'Don't come into my painting.'

PAINTING BRIDGES *Features*

I have chosen four attractive and interesting bridge styles for you to consider here, with a step-by-step diagram showing how to draw a simple bridge.

Sketch of Linn of Dee nr Braemar Scotland

I completed this quick demonstration sketch in water-soluble crayons when I was tutoring a painting holiday at Braemar in Scotland. The bridge is the famous Linn of Dee, a popular tourist attraction. Constructed from blocks of stone, it creates a pleasing, functional design over a gorge with fast-flowing water.

I used water-soluble crayons washed in with brushstrokes to create this simple representation. Water-soluble crayons are ideal for sketching and painting outdoors. I always carry a small tin of ten. This can be tucked into a pocket and all you need in addition is a brush to produce quick 'doodles'. The rocks were created by moving wet paint with a palette knife.

This bridge is typical of those found in many states of North America. They are simple, functional, wooden structures that are partially covered. Note the variety of colours used to paint the woodwork.

'Clapper' bridges are simple in form, crudely constructed and rough in appearance. They were one of the first types of bridge, made by placing large slabs of rock across a river or beck, and were used prior to the use of arches in bridge building. Examples can be found in most counties of England; this one is at Postbridge in Devon.

HOW TO DRAW A BRIDGE

Drawing a bridge can be very simple if you know the correct procedure – just follow the steps shown below.

This simple river scene spanned by a bridge was drawn using the procedure shown above and described below.

1. Draw a rectangle. Divide the rectangle into four equal parts by drawing one vertical and one horizontal line through its centre.
2. Draw two further rectangles, one each side of the large one.
3. Divide the large rectangle into eight equal parts by drawing a vertical line in each half.
4. Divide each of the two outer areas of the large rectangle in two by drawing two further vertical lines.
5. Draw a horizontal line to represent the top of the arch by dividing the top area in half horizontally.
6. Draw two equally placed vertical lines to represent the width of the bottom of the arch.
7. Draw in the arch itself.
8. Draw in the general shape of the bridge. Note the angle at the base of the left side of the arch.

PAINTING WALLS *Features and textures*

A newly built stone wall is a pleasure to behold. Stone walls come in many imaginative designs, depending on the requirements and skills of the farmer, who will use the natural materials available to him. If the wall is near a river, rounded stones are used; if it is near a quarry, natural slivers of slate/stone may be chosen. The waller may incorporate flat stones and project them from the wall at various points to make steps which allow it to be scaled.

The techniques discussed here would also be used for painting bridges.

This wall has been built using large stones unearthed from land clearance. To capture it, I applied Raw Sienna wet into wet over a weak Payne's Gray underpainting. When this was dry, I used Burnt Umber to paint in the darker stones and shadows.

There are two interesting features in this wall: a hole, known as a 'hogg' hole (incorporated to allow young sheep known as 'hoggs' pass through), and a large stone which enables the gate to be fastened.

A 'flag wall' is created by positioning large stone or slate slabs in the ground. This type of wall is often seen around churches and gardens, or is used to denote boundaries. I used various tones of Payne's Gray to create texture.

For this brick wall I applied first a Raw Sienna/Alizarin Crimson under-painting and while it was still wet dropped in Burnt Sienna, Payne's Gray and Vermilion, allowing the colours to merge together. When the paint was approximately one-third dry, I used a tissue to create light areas on the bricks. When it was completely dry, I painted shadows along the left-hand and lower edges of each brick to create a three-dimensional appearance.

A palette knife helped me to create this painting of a stone wall. After applying a Raw Sienna wash I brushed in Burnt Sienna with dark tones of a Payne's Gray/Alizarin Crimson mix wet into wet. I waited until this was about one-third dry before moving the paint with the palette knife to create the stone structure and the coping stones.

Watercolour and oil pastel can combine well to create texture. In this example the wall was painted initially with a cream-coloured oil pastel and then over-painted with watercolours. After applying the usual Raw Sienna wash, I used Burnt Sienna, Burnt Umber and a Payne's Gray/Alizarin Crimson mix, and when this was dry painted shadows on two edges of selected stones.

Useful colours for painting bridges and walls

Burnt Umber

French Ultramarine
Alizarin Crimson

Vermilion
Burnt Sienna

Raw Sienna

Payne's Gray

Burnt Sienna
Burnt Umber

Payne's Gray
Alizarin Crimson

PAINTING BRIDGES *Close up*

This atmospheric scene was painted in acrylic watercolours at **Wasdale Head** in the English Lake District. The farmstead and lovely stone bridge make it a pleasing composition. In the background is Kirk Fell, its peak shrouded in low cloud, and next to it Great Gable, which is partly obscured behind the trees.

The public house in Wasdale is the 'gathering hole' for those setting out to climb either of these local land-marks. The well-worn track they take can be seen in the painting.

FELL AND SKY

In this painting I particularly wanted to capture the effect of the cloud around the top of Kirk Fell. The cloud was so low that the fell was barely visible. I painted the fell first, using directional strokes with a hake brush. After applying a Raw Sienna wash, and while it was still wet, I brushed in various greens, following the structure of the mountain. While the paint was still wet, I painted in the sky, allowing the paint to run over the top of the fell. With a tissue I removed paint to create the effect of cloud over the peak of the fell.

FOLIAGE AND FOREGROUND

The detailed bushes and specimen trees were painted by stippling in the dark under-painting, using a Payne's Gray/Permanent Sap Green mix. When this was dry, lighter groups of foliage were stippled in using an old bristle brush loaded with various tones of green.

The rough foreground was painted using the same techniques as that for the trees. When the paint was dry, a Raw Sienna/Burnt Sienna glaze (a small amount of paint and lots of water) was washed over the near foreground to add colour and sparkle. The grazing sheep were then painted.

170

BRIDGE AND WATER

The bridge is very simple to paint, using angular strokes with a rigger brush. The colours used were Raw Sienna and Burnt Sienna, with Payne's Gray added for the shadows. Take care to ensure your bridge is a pleasing shape. Paint in a little of the underside of the bridge. The stones were painted using a size 6 round brush. and the water painted

using a Payne's Gray/Cerulean Blue mix, leaving areas of white paper uncovered. A hake brush was used for the water. When the painting was completed, a Raw Sienna glaze was selectively applied to areas on the fell, the distant fields, the trees and in the water – just small amounts here and there to add sparkle to the painting.

PAINTING BRIDGES and WALLS *Project*

Brougham Castle near Penrith in the English Lake District lies on the banks of the River Eamont. The castle was built between the 12th and 13th centuries. The sturdy stone bridge spanning the river provides a majestic foreground to the castle. The atmospheric sky and distribution of light over the castle walls and the fast-flowing water made the painting of this evening scene irresistible.

1. PRELIMINARIES
The outline drawing was prepared taking care that the correct proportions with regard to height and width of the castle were represented correctly. Similarly, the bridge structure was drawn, the width and profile of the arches being the most important considerations.

The sky is a special feature in this painting. An initial wash of Raw Sienna was applied using a hake brush. While this was less than one-third dry, the cloud structures were brushed in using mixes made from Burnt Sienna, Payne's Gray and Cerulean Blue. These colours were also used to paint the water. I took care to leave some of the paper uncovered to represent flow patterns and applied pale Raw Sienna washes to represent highlights on the water.

2. STONEWORK
The castle's stonework was painted by applying an initial pale Raw Sienna wash over all the walls, with small touches of Burnt Sienna brushed in while this was still wet. When dry a mix of Payne's Gray and Alizarin Crimson was used to paint the shadows on the castle walls, the profile of the windows and the arrow slits. The grass in the foreground was painted using a soft green, and the shadows painted taking care to leave the white of the paper uncovered to represent the track leading to the main gate. Similar colours and techniques to those for the castle's stonework were used for the bridge. When the paint was approximately one-third dry, a palette knife was used to scratch in the impressions of stonework. When the paint was completely dry the side and bottom of selected stones were darkened using a Payne's Gray/Alizarin Crimson mix to represent shadows.

3. TREES
The distant trees were painted next, using mixes of Raw Sienna, Permanent Sap Green for the darker tones. The foreground trees were similarly painted, using a stippling action with an old bristle brush. A few tree structures were scratched in with a palette knife and cocktail stick. Some darker tones were added to the water under the trees to give depth to the painting. A rigger brush was used to give fine detail to the fence in the distance.

4. ADDING THE DETAILS

It's time to bring the painting together and add the finishing touches. Raw Sienna, Cadmium Yellow Pale and Burnt Sienna glazes were applied to the foliage and tree structures. These same glazes were also used to colour the rocks and create depth of tone.

Highlights to the foliage were then applied. Paper masks had to be first cut to shape to protect other areas, such as the sky; I used a piece of mounting card cut to various profiles to fit around the trees. To apply the paint, I took an old toothbrush, dipped it in Cadmium Yellow Pale, ran my thumb over the bristles and then spattered the colour onto the foliage.

Techniques and tips

• Masking is useful for protecting areas of white paper you wish to preserve. Over-painting will be repelled by the masking. Once the paint is dry, the masking is removed with a putty eraser.

• Wet into wet or wet into damp techniques are useful for textured effects.
• Rough-textured surfaces or flaking plaster are best created by blotting with an absorbent tissue or kitchen roll and using a rigger brush to paint in shadows, indicating the edge of the plaster and cracks in the surface.

The colours used

| Payne's Gray | Alizarin Crimson | Raw Sienna | Cerulean Blue | Cadmium Yellow Pale | Permanent Sap Green | Burnt Sienna |

Eilean Donan is Scotland's most recognizable castle and a source of inspiration for generations of artists. The castle has been a fortified site for at least eight hundred years, although the present castle was restored in the early 20th century. Eilean Donan and its magnificent setting attracts visitors world wide. The castle has been the venue for many films, notably *Highlander*, starring Sean Connery, and *The Master of Ballintrae* with Errol Flynn.

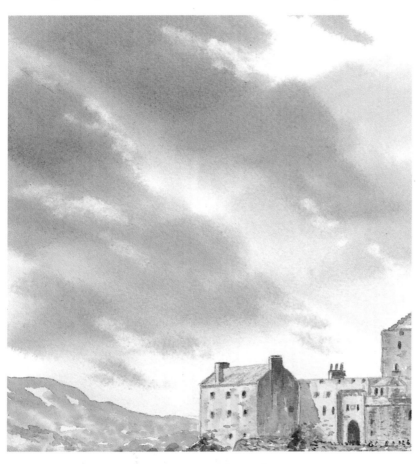

SKY AND MOUNTAINS

A piece of ³/₄ in masking tape was positioned across the paper to represent the water-line. The sky was painted using a 1½ in hake brush by initially applying a pale Raw Sienna wash and creating the cloud formations by brushing in mixes from Payne's Gray, Cerulean Blue and Alizarin Crimson. A tissue was used to soften cloud edges and create an interesting cloud study.

When the sky was dry, the distant mountains were painted using various tones of the same mixes used for the sky. When these were dry, the masking tape was carefully removed.

BUILDINGS AND WATER

I took care when preparing the initial outline drawing to ensure the buildings were drawn correctly. When painting buildings from a distance, I find the use of a small pair of binoculars invaluable. In this example, there are so many variations in the design of the building, I needed the binoculars to determine some of the features, particularly as the shadows, so important in this scene, tended to make observation with the naked eye difficult.

The buildings were painted by applying a Raw Sienna wash overall and brushing in a little Burnt Umber and a Payne's Gray/Alizarin Crimson mix.

The shadows were painted once the under-painting was dry, as were the windows and darker features. The tonal values of the shadows were important in this landscape.

Horizontal strokes with the side of a size 14 round brush were used to paint the water, with sparkle added by means of lighter touches. I painted the rocks after completing the bridge and water.

Tonal Studies

Use tonal value studies to determine your best viewpoint. These studies help to establish your values – lights and darks – prior to applying paint.

THE BRIDGE

From my chosen viewpoint the arches of the bridge linking the castle to the mainland had to be carefully drawn, as did the supporting bridge, towers and buttresses. Care was taken to observe and capture the shadows on the arches. The bridge is quite simple in structure, but from my viewpoint it was a tricky exercise to draw, in particular its relationship with the stone wall surrounding the path and leading to the castle entrance. The colours and techniques used were similar to those for the main buildings.

I added a few figures walking to the castle; at the time I painted the scene there were far too many people to include.

PORTRAIT OF THE ARTIST

Keith Fenwick is one of the UK's leading teachers of painting techniques. He enjoys a tremendous following among leisure painters, who flock to his demonstrations and workshops at major fine art and craft shows.

Keith is a Chartered Engineer, a Fellow of the Royal Society of Arts, an Advisory Panel member of the Society for All Artists and holds several professional qualifications including an honours degree. He served an engineering apprenticeship, becoming chief draughtsman, before progressing to senior management in both industry and further education. He took early retirement from his position as Associate Principal/Director of Sites and Publicity at one of the UK's largest colleges of further education in order to devote more time to his great love, landscape painting.

Keith's paintings are in collections in the United Kingdom and other European countries, as well as in the United States, Canada, New Zealand, Australia, Japan and the Middle East.

Keith runs painting holidays in the UK and Europe, seminars and workshops nationwide and demonstrates to up to 50 art societies each year. Keith can be seen demonstrating painting techniques at most major fine art and craft shows in the UK. He has had a long and fruitful association with Winsor & Newton, for whom he is a principal demonstrator.

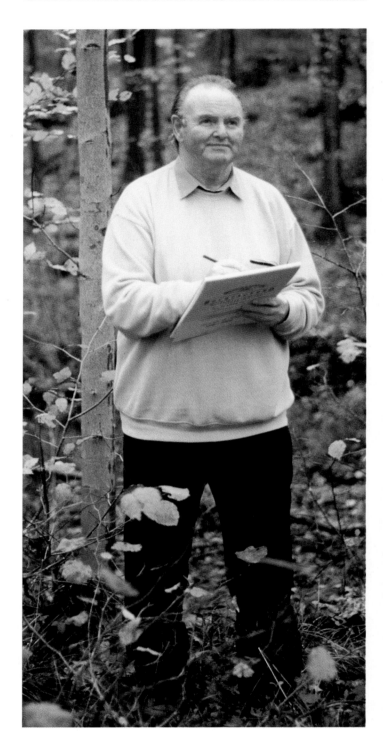

Keith's expertise in landscape painting, his writings, teaching, video-making and broadcasting ensure an understanding of student needs. His book *Seasonal Landscapes* has proved very popular, as have his 20 best-selling art teaching videos, which have benefited students worldwide. He is a regular contributor to art and craft magazines.

Keith finds great satisfaction in encouraging those who have always wanted to paint but lack the confidence to have a go, as well as helping more experienced painters to develop their skills further. He hopes this series will be a constant companion to those wishing to improve their skills and experiment with new ways to paint the landscape.